Dear Readers,

I am excited and proud to share our 2023 catalog with you. Engage Books strives to publish books that make a difference, books that help children think critically about the world. Our goal is to help children become informed and engaged citizens who can make the world a better place. Our frontlist of 46 new Level 1, 2, and 3 readers was created in the hope of achieving this goal.

Our flagship series, Understand Your Mind and Body, teaches kids about *Autism, ADHD, Anxiety, Depression,* and *Dyslexia,* and gives seven- to-nine-year-olds the opportunity to understand how their own minds, or the minds of loved ones, functions. Books on *Asthma, Diabetes, Obesity,* and *Vision Loss* help kids to recognize changes that may be happening their bodies.

It is vital that we empower the next generation to recognize the mistakes in our past. Our Working Towards Equality series teaches kids about *Antisemitism, Homophobia, Racism,* and *Sexism* in the hopes that we can help foster a kinder and gentler future.

Following a pandemic, it is more important than ever that we help children to navigate complex emotions. In our Emotions and Feelings series, we teach children about *Fear, Guilt, Happiness, Worry,* and *Anger* while recognizing the *Gratitude, Sadness,* and *Grief* that many are facing. By understanding their emotions, children can begin to heal.

We believe in speaking to children as creative and imaginative individuals who may one day change the world. Our Changing Planet is a series that pulls back the curtain on subjects like *Air Pollution, Climate Change, Extreme Weather,* and *Habitat Loss.* We hope that by informing children about these issues, we can inspire them to come up with solutions as they grow older.

Sincerely,

Alexis Roumanis | B.A., M.Pub.
President | Engage Books

Contact
P: 1.604.551.0769
E: alexis@engagebooks.ca
WWW.ENGAGEBOOKS.COM

Explore our books at:
WWW.ENGAGEBOOKS.COM

Explore our books at:
WWW.ENGAGEBOOKS.COM

LEVEL Pre-1 **Beginner reader**

Level Pre-1 readers are aimed at children who are starting to read.
Basic language, word repetition, and short, simple sentences help kids read
with confidence.

LEVEL 1 **Reading together**

Level 1 readers are aimed at children who are starting to recognize common
words and are capable of sounding out unfamiliar words. Short, simple
sentences help guide the reader through new concepts and ideas.

LEVEL 2 **Reading with help**

Level 2 readers are aimed at children who are becoming more confident at
reading on their own. Simple sentences and informative captions help readers
understand new ideas, while key words increase readers' vocabularies.

LEVEL 3 **Reading independently**

Level 3 readers are aimed at children who are reading by themselves and can
grasp new concepts. Key words and captions help readers understand new
vocabulary and more challenging sentence structure.

BINDING KEY
PB: Paperback
HC: Hardcover case laminate over board

RIGHTS KEY
WD: World rights available

This project has been
made possible in part by the
Government of Canada.

Canada

Contents

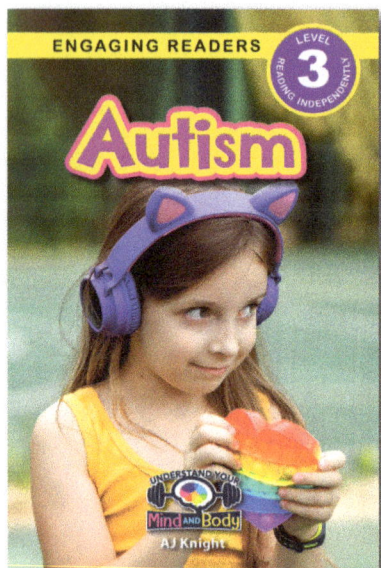

Autism is not a disease or an illness. People with autism think, act, and communicate differently than non-autistic people. Some autistic people do not speak. Others may get overwhelmed easily. Learn about the ways that people with autism adapt to living in a world that often fails to understand them.

DETAILS

Pub Date: August 2023
Size: 6x9 in • 152 x 229 mm
Age: 6 - 9
Grades: 2 - 4
Pages: 32
Rights: WD

FORMATS

PB: 978-1-77476-777-1
US $5.99
HC: 978-1-77476-776-4
US $24.99
EPUB: 978-1-77476-778-8
US $4.99
PDF: 978-1-77476-779-5
US $4.99
Audio: 978-1-77476-434-3
US $4.99

No two people experience ADHD the same way. It can make it hard to focus or hard to keep still. ADHD is a complicated condition that affects people of all ages. Find out why it's important to get a diagnosis and how to be a good friend to someone who has ADHD.

DETAILS

Pub Date: August 2023
Size: 6x9 in • 152 x 229 mm
Age: 6 - 9
Grades: 2 - 4
Pages: 32
Rights: WD

FORMATS

PB: 978-1-77476-785-6
US $5.99
HC: 978-1-77476-784-9
US $24.99
EPUB: 978-1-77476-786-3
US $4.99
PDF: 978-1-77476-787-0
US $4.99
Audio: 978-1-77878-105-6
US $4.99

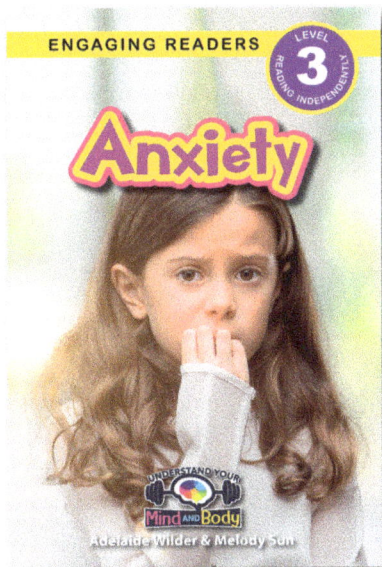

Most people feel anxious from time to time. But for some people, anxiety can be extreme and constant. Anxiety can cause panic attacks, constant worry, and fear. Find out how people with anxiety can learn to deal with their symptoms, and how you can help someone with anxiety.

DETAILS
Pub Date: August 2023
Size: 6x9 in • 152 x 229 mm
Age: 6 - 9
Grades: 2 - 4
Pages: 32
Rights: WD

FORMATS
PB: 978-1-77476-773-3
US $5.99
HC: 978-1-77476-772-6
US $24.99
EPUB: 978-1-77476-774-0
US $4.99
PDF: 978-1-77476-775-7
US $4.99
Audio: 978-1-77878-106-3
US $4.99

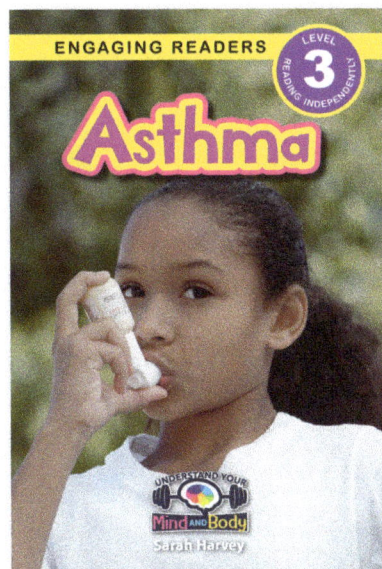

Having asthma can be scary. But it doesn't have to stop you from leading an active life. It helps to know more about the disease and how it is treated. Find out what you can do to take care of yourself if you have asthma and how you can help others who have it too.

DETAILS
Pub Date: August 2023
Size: 6x9 in • 152 x 229 mm
Age: 6 - 9
Grades: 2 - 4
Pages: 32
Rights: WD

FORMATS
PB: 978-1-77476-872-3
US $5.99
HC: 978-1-77476-871-6
US $24.99
EPUB: 978-1-77476-873-0
US $4.99
PDF: 978-1-77476-874-7
US $4.99
Audio: 978-1-77878-107-0
US $4.99

ENGAGING READERS

LEVEL 3 READING INDEPENDENTLY

Body Image

UNDERSTAND YOUR Mind AND Body

Adelaide Wilder & Ashley Lee

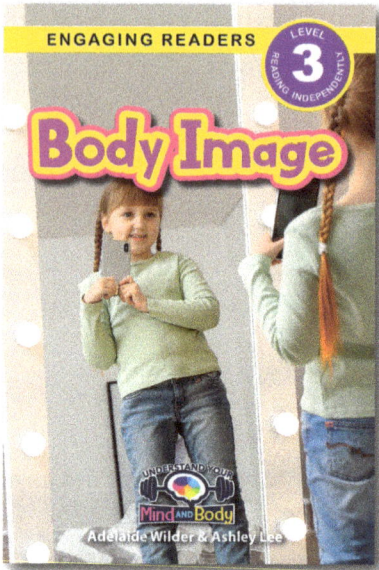

Body image issues can be overwhelming. Many people–old and young, male and female–struggle with them. That's why it's so important to look beyond appearances and celebrate what makes people unique. Find out what causes body image issues and how you can help someone who is struggling.

DETAILS
Pub Date: August 2023
Size: 6x9 in • 152 x 229 mm
Age: 6 - 9
Grades: 2 - 4
Pages: 32
Rights: WD

FORMATS
PB: 978-1-77476-781-8
US $5.99
HC: 978-1-77476-780-1
US $24.99
EPUB: 978-1-77476-782-5
US $4.99
PDF: 978-1-77476-783-2
US $4.99
Audio: 978-1-77878-108-7
US $4.99

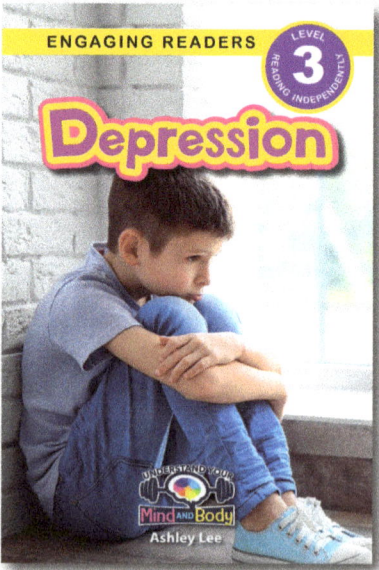

ENGAGING READERS

LEVEL 3 READING INDEPENDENTLY

Depression

UNDERSTAND YOUR Mind AND Body

Ashley Lee

Depression is a mental illness that can affect the way you think, feel, and behave. Depression is more than just feeling sad. Find out what exactly depression is and what can be done to make a depressed person feel better.

DETAILS
Pub Date: August 2023
Size: 6x9 in • 152 x 229 mm
Age: 6 - 9
Grades: 2 - 4
Pages: 32
Rights: WD

FORMATS
PB: 978-1-77476-677-4
US $5.99
HC: 978-1-77476-676-7
US $24.99
EPUB: 978-1-77476-678-1
US $4.99
PDF: 978-1-77476-679-8
US $4.99
Audio: 978-1-77878-109-4
US $4.99

ENGAGING READERS

LEVEL
3
READING INDEPENDENTLY

Diabetes

UNDERSTAND YOUR
Mind and Body
Kit Caudron-Robinson

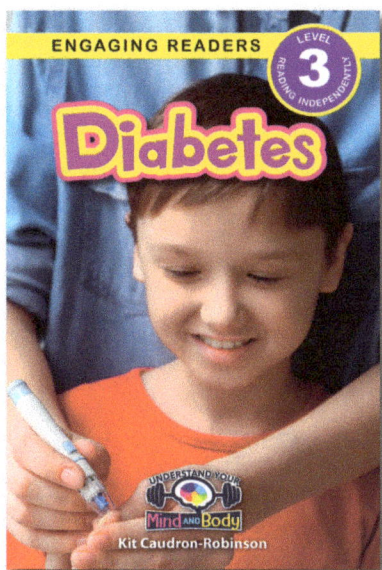

More and more children are living with diabetes. Diabetes can cause many types of serious health problems. Learn the difference between Type 1 and Type 2 diabetes and how to take care of yourself if you have either type. Small changes in diet and activity level can make a huge difference to diabetics.

DETAILS
Pub Date: August 2023
Size: 6x9 in • 152 x 229 mm
Age: 6 - 9
Grades: 2 - 4
Pages: 32
Rights: WD

FORMATS
PB: 978-1-77476-979-9
US $5.99
HC: 978-1-77476-978-2
US $24.99
EPUB: 978-1-77476-980-5
US $4.99
PDF: 978-1-77476-981-2
US $4.99
Audio: 978-1-77878-110-0
US $4.99

ENGAGING READERS

LEVEL
3
READING INDEPENDENTLY

Dyslexia

UNDERSTAND YOUR
Mind and Body
Sarah Harvey

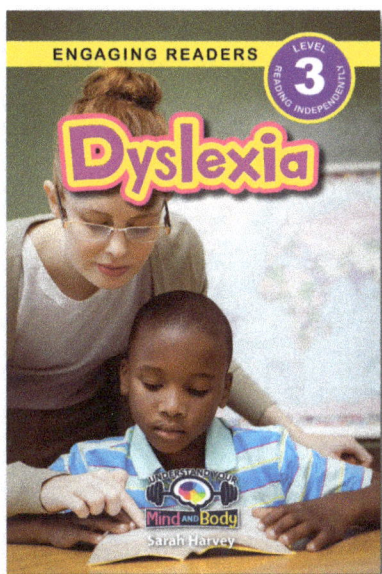

Dyslexia is a learning disability that makes reading, writing, and spelling difficult. It has nothing to do with intelligence. One in five people have dyslexia. Learn how dyslexia is identified and what kinds of strategies help people who have it.

DETAILS
Pub Date: August 2023
Size: 6x9 in • 152 x 229 mm
Age: 6 - 9
Grades: 2 - 4
Pages: 32
Rights: WD

FORMATS
PB: 978-1-77878-166-7
US $5.99
HC: 978-1-77878-165-0
US $24.99
EPUB: 978-1-77878-167-4
US $4.99
PDF: 978-1-77878-168-1
US $4.99
Audio: 978-1-77878-111-7
US $4.99

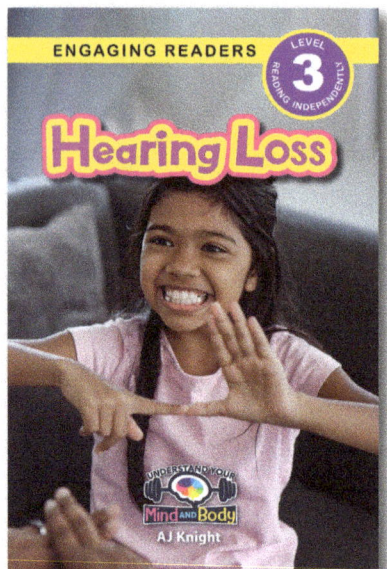

ENGAGING READERS

LEVEL 3 READING INDEPENDENTLY

Hearing Loss

Mind AND Body

AJ Knight

Hearing loss doesn't only affect older people. It has many causes and can be mild or severe. Learn about how the ear works and what you can do to protect your ears. Find out about new technologies that are improving the lives of people with hearing loss.

DETAILS
Pub Date: August 2023
Size: 6x9 in • 152 x 229 mm
Age: 6 - 9
Grades: 2 - 4
Pages: 32
Rights: WD

FORMATS
PB: 978-1-77878-170-4
US $5.99
HC: 978-1-77878-169-8
US $24.99
EPUB: 978-1-77878-171-1
US $4.99
PDF: 978-1-77878-172-8
US $4.99
Audio: 978-1-77878-112-4
US $4.99

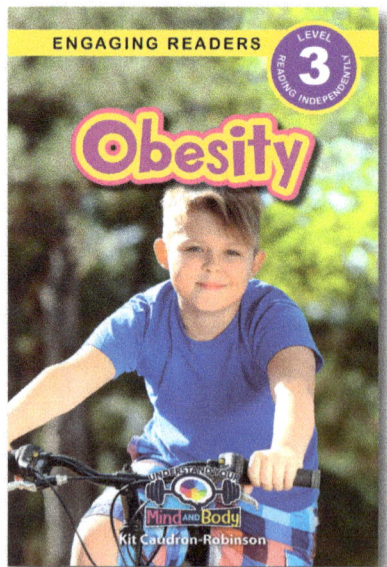

ENGAGING READERS

LEVEL 3 READING INDEPENDENTLY

Obesity

Mind AND Body

Kit Caudron-Robinson

Over 370 million children and adolescents in the world are obese. Obesity is a disease that can affect both physical and mental health. Learn what can be done to prevent and treat obesity and promote healthy lifestyles.

DETAILS
Pub Date: August 2023
Size: 6x9 in • 152 x 229 mm
Age: 6 - 9
Grades: 2 - 4
Pages: 32
Rights: WD

FORMATS
PB: 978-1-77476-975-1
US $5.99
HC: 978-1-77476-974-4
US $24.99
EPUB: 978-1-77476-976-8
US $4.99
PDF: 978-1-77476-977-5
US $4.99
Audio: 978-1-77878-113-1
US $4.99

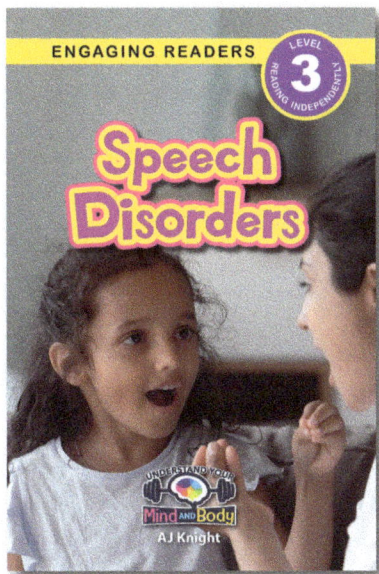

Most of us take it for granted that we can speak well enough to be understood. But what if you are one of the many kids who have a speech disorder? Find out what a speech disorder is, how it is treated, and why it is so important to understand the challenges that come with it.

DETAILS
Pub Date: August 2023
Size: 6x9 in • 152 x 229 mm
Age: 6 - 9
Grades: 2 - 4
Pages: 32
Rights: WD

FORMATS
PB: 978-1-77476-793-1
US $5.99
HC: 978-1-77476-792-4
US $24.99
EPUB: 978-1-77476-794-8
US $4.99
PDF: 978-1-77476-795-5
US $4.99
Audio: 978-1-77878-114-8
US $4.99

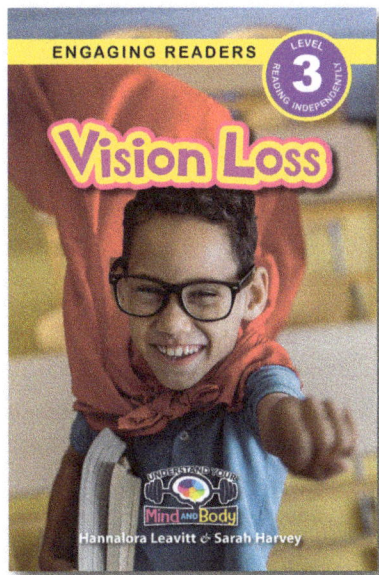

Vision loss does not mean total blindness. It can be mild or severe. Eighty percent of vision loss can be prevented or treated. People with vision loss lead full and active lives. Find out what causes vision loss, why it's important to get regular eye exams, and what you can do to help someone with vision loss.

DETAILS
Pub Date: August 2023
Size: 6x9 in • 152 x 229 mm
Age: 6 - 9
Grades: 2 - 4
Pages: 32
Rights: WD

FORMATS
PB: 978-1-77476-789-4
US $5.99
HC: 978-1-77476-788-7
US $24.99
EPUB: 978-1-77476-790-0
US $4.99
PDF: 978-1-77476-791-7
US $4.99
Audio: 978-1-77878-115-5
US $4.99

LEVEL 3 READING INDEPENDENTLY

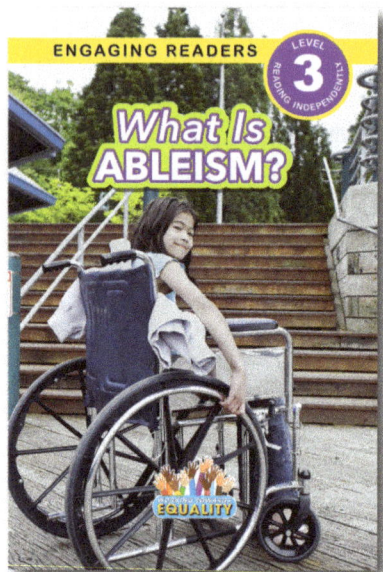

Ableism judges and excludes people who live with disabilities based simply on their disability. Education and awareness are key to understanding disability. Learn how to recognize ableism, and figure out what you can do to be more inclusive.

DETAILS

Pub Date: August 2023
Size: 6x9 in • 152 x 229 mm
Age: 6 - 9
Grades: 2 - 4
Pages: 32
Rights: WD

FORMATS

PB: 978-1-77476-856-3
US $5.99
HC: 978-1-77476-855-6
US $24.99
EPUB: 978-1-77476-857-0
US $4.99
PDF: 978-1-77476-858-7
US $4.99
Audio: 978-1-77878-127-8
US $4.99

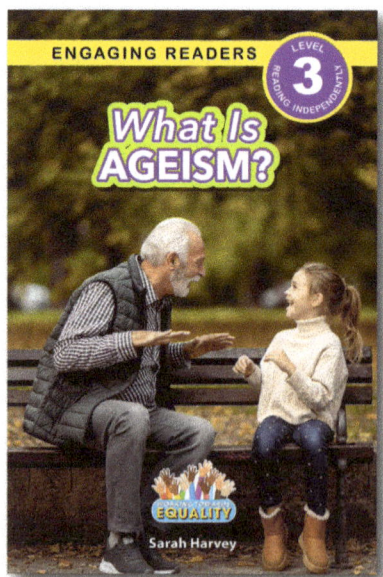

Ageism is discrimination against a certain age group. It mostly affects older people, who are often ignored or dismissed because of their age. Younger people can experience ageism as well. Find out how to spot ageism and what you can do to help end it in your community.

DETAILS

Pub Date: August 2023
Size: 6x9 in • 152 x 229 mm
Age: 6 - 9
Grades: 2 - 4
Pages: 32
Rights: WD

FORMATS

PB: 978-1-77476-868-6
US $5.99
HC: 978-1-77476-867-9
US $24.99
EPUB: 978-1-77476-869-3
US $4.99
PDF: 978-1-77476-870-9
US $4.99
Audio: 978-1-77878-128-5
US $4.99

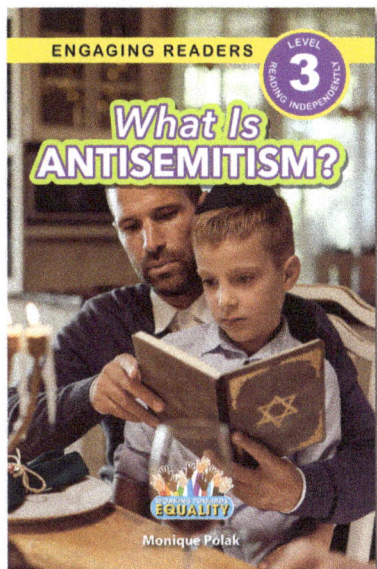

Anti-semitic hate groups have been persecuting Jews for a very long time. The most famous historical instance of anti-semitism was the Holocaust. Anti-semitism is on the rise in the world. It's more important than ever to understand what it is and how you can stand up against it.

DETAILS
Pub Date: August 2023
Size: 6x9 in • 152 x 229 mm
Age: 6 - 9
Grades: 2 - 4
Pages: 32
Rights: WD

FORMATS
PB: 978-1-77476-864-8
US $5.99
HC: 978-1-77476-863-1
US $24.99
EPUB: 978-1-77476-865-5
US $4.99
PDF: 978-1-77476-866-2
US $4.99
Audio: 978-1-77878-129-2
US $4.99

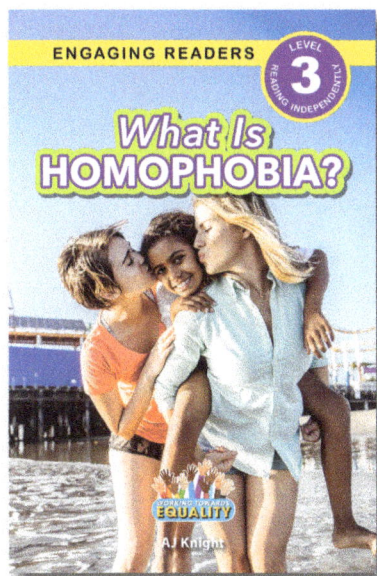

It's likely that you have already witnessed homophobia and transphobia. The hatred and prejudice directed at people within the LGBTQIA+ community is hard to miss. Learn how to spot homophobic and transphobic language and behavior. Become an ally. It is a powerful thing to do in the face of hate.

DETAILS
Pub Date: August 2023
Size: 6x9 in • 152 x 229 mm
Age: 6 - 9
Grades: 2 - 4
Pages: 32
Rights: WD

FORMATS
PB: 978-1-77476-860-0
US $5.99
HC: 978-1-77476-859-4
US $24.99
EPUB: 978-1-77476-861-7
US $4.99
PDF: 978-1-77476-862-4
US $4.99
Audio: 978-1-77878-130-8
US $4.99

LEVEL 3 READING INDEPENDENTLY

WORKING TOWARDS EQUALITY

What Is RACISM?

ENGAGING READERS — LEVEL 3 READING INDEPENDENTLY

Sarah Harvey & Melody Sun

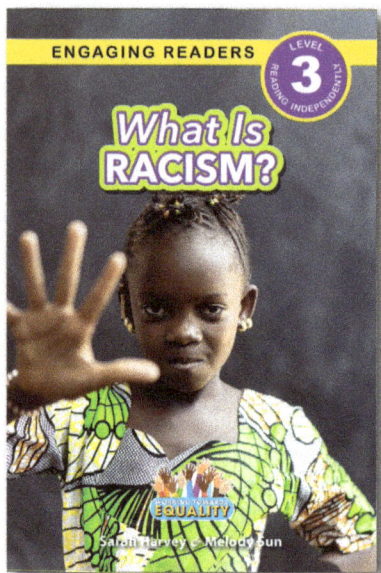

Talking about racism is hard. Often people just don't know what to say, so they say nothing. It's important to learn what racism is (and isn't). Find out why some people are racist and what you can do if you see or experience racism. The more information you have, the more ready you will be to stand up to racism.

DETAILS

Pub Date: August 2023
Size: 6x9 in • 152 x 229 mm
Age: 6 - 9
Grades: 2 - 4
Pages: 32
Rights: WD

FORMATS

PB: 978-1-77476-848-8
US $5.99
HC: 978-1-77476-847-1
US $24.99
EPUB: 978-1-77476-849-5
US $4.99
PDF: 978-1-77476-850-1
US $4.99
Audio: 978-1-77878-131-5
US $4.99

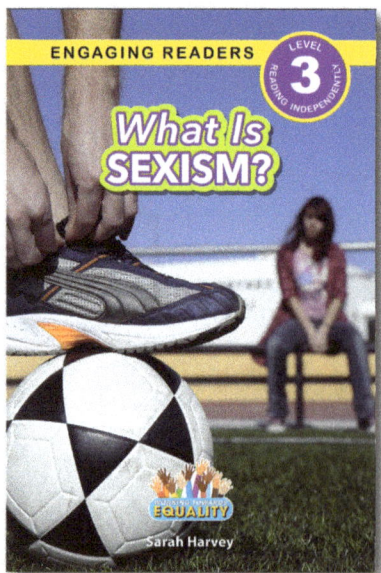

What Is SEXISM?

ENGAGING READERS — LEVEL 3 READING INDEPENDENTLY

EQUALITY

Sarah Harvey

Sexism is something you learn, not something you are born with. It's at school, at work and even at home sometimes. Movies, books, TV, and social media are full of sexist content. It's important to learn how to identify sexism. That way you can stand up to it and help others do the same.

DETAILS

Pub Date: August 2023
Size: 6x9 in • 152 x 229 mm
Age: 6 - 9
Grades: 2 - 4
Pages: 32
Rights: WD

FORMATS

PB: 978-1-77476-852-5
US $5.99
HC: 978-1-77476-851-8
US $24.99
EPUB: 978-1-77476-853-2
US $4.99
PDF: 978-1-77476-854-9
US $4.99
Audio: 978-1-77878-132-2
US $4.99

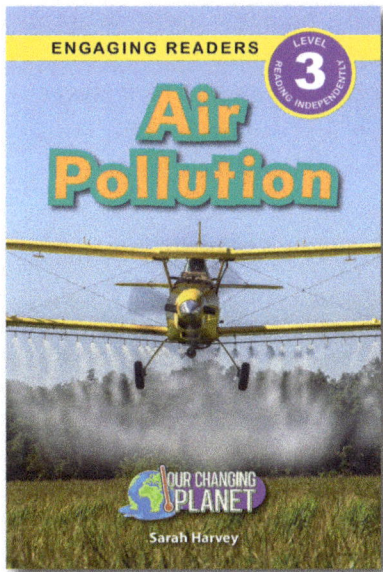

It's hard to escape air pollution these days. Exhaust from cars and trucks, smoke from factories and wildfires, and even dust and pollen can make it hard to breathe. Air pollution is one of the causes of climate change. Find out what is being done to reduce air pollution and make the planet a cleaner, safer place.

DETAILS
Pub Date: August 2023
Size: 6x9 in • 152 x 229 mm
Age: 6 - 9
Grades: 2 - 4
Pages: 32
Rights: WD

FORMATS
PB: 978-1-77476-888-4
US $5.99
HC: 978-1-77476-887-7
US $24.99
EPUB: 978-1-77476-889-1
US $4.99
PDF: 978-1-77476-890-7
US $4.99
Audio: 978-1-77878-121-6
US $4.99

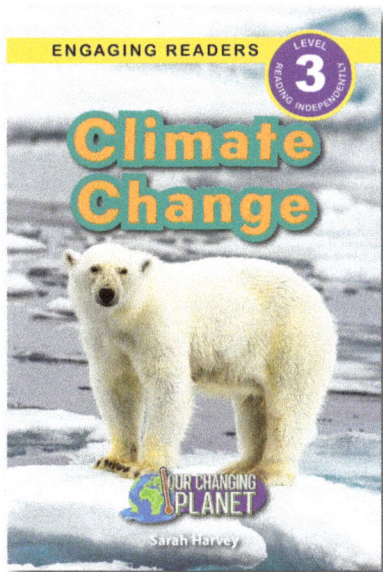

Climate change is harming our beautiful planet. It's hard not to feel scared and discouraged. But it's not too late to help Earth heal. Find out what is being done to slow down climate change and what you can do to help.

DETAILS
Pub Date: August 2023
Size: 6x9 in • 152 x 229 mm
Age: 6 - 9
Grades: 2 - 4
Pages: 32
Rights: WD

FORMATS
PB: 978-1-77476-884-6
US $5.99
HC: 978-1-77476-883-9
US $24.99
EPUB: 978-1-77476-885-3
US $4.99
PDF: 978-1-77476-886-0
US $4.99
Audio: 978-1-77878-122-3
US $4.99

ENGAGING READERS — LEVEL 3 READING INDEPENDENTLY

Extreme Weather

OUR CHANGING PLANET

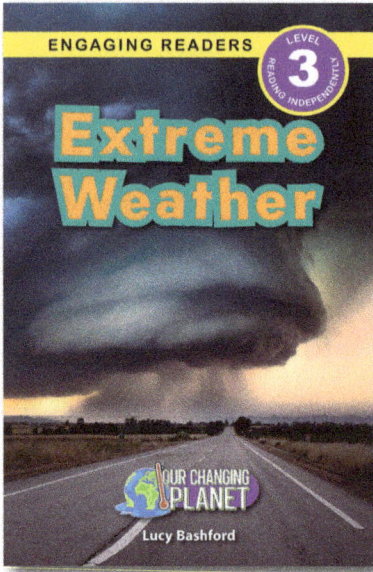

Lucy Bashford

When does weather become extreme weather? How is it related to climate change? Find out what extreme weather is and why it is becoming more frequent and dangerous. Learn what a black blizzard is and why there has been a drought in Chile for 13 years.

DETAILS
Pub Date: August 2023
Size: 6x9 in • 152 x 229 mm
Age: 6 - 9
Grades: 2 - 4
Pages: 32
Rights: WD

FORMATS
PB: 978-1-77476-995-9
US $5.99
HC: 978-1-77476-994-2
US $24.99
EPUB: 978-1-77476-996-6
US $4.99
PDF: 978-1-77476-997-3
US $4.99
Audio: 978-1-77878-125-4
US $4.99

ENGAGING READERS — LEVEL 3 READING INDEPENDENTLY

Habitat Loss

OUR CHANGING PLANET

Lucy Bashford

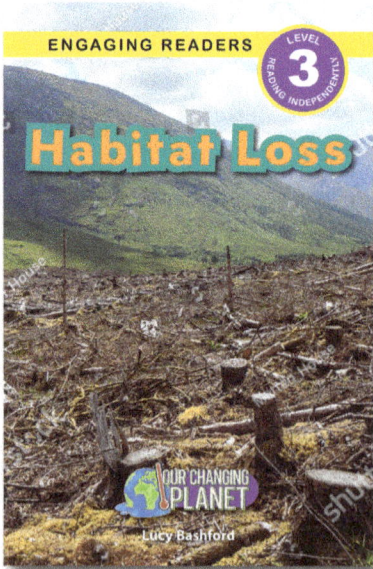

Habitat loss is having a huge effect on Earth's plants and animals. When habitats are lost, so are ecosystems. Humans need healthy ecosystems for clean air and water, for medicines, and for our emotional well-being. Many people are working hard to restore and preserve habitats. Find out what you can do to keep Earth healthy too.

DETAILS
Pub Date: August 2023
Size: 6x9 in • 152 x 229 mm
Age: 6 - 9
Grades: 2 - 4
Pages: 32
Rights: WD

FORMATS
PB: 978-1-77476-904-1
US $5.99
HC: 978-1-77476-903-4
US $24.99
EPUB: 978-1-77476-905-8
US $4.99
PDF: 978-1-77476-906-5
US $4.99
Audio: 978-1-77878-124-7
US $4.99

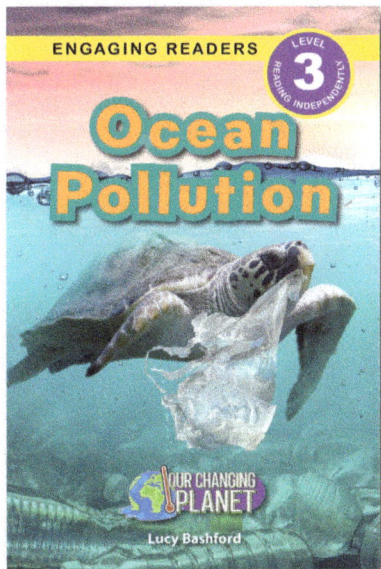

Humans have polluted the ocean with plastics, chemicals, garbage, and oil spills. It's time for us to stop throwing our waste in the ocean. Learn what is being done to clean up the ocean and to protect marine life.

DETAILS

Pub Date: August 2023
Size: 6x9 in • 152 x 229 mm
Age: 6 - 9
Grades: 2 - 4
Pages: 32
Rights: WD

FORMATS

PB: 978-1-77476-995-9
US $5.99
HC: 978-1-77476-994-2
US $24.99
EPUB: 978-1-77476-996-6
US $4.99
PDF: 978-1-77476-997-3
US $4.99
Audio: 978-1-77878-125-4
US $4.99

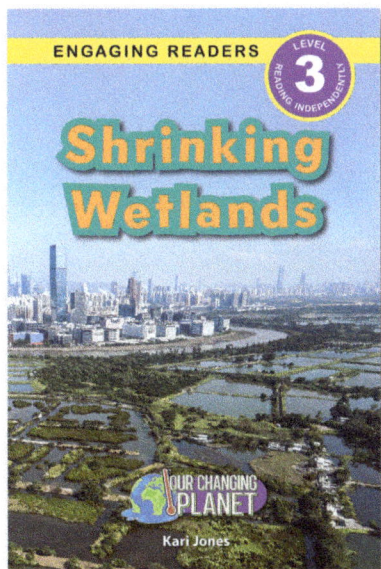

Some wetlands are on coasts, some are inland. Marshes, bogs, and swamps are all wetlands. Wherever they are, they are full of plant and animal life. They also fight climate change. But wetlands are in danger from development and pollution. Find out what is being done to preserve these vital parts of our environment.

DETAILS

Pub Date: August 2023
Size: 6x9 in • 152 x 229 mm
Age: 6 - 9
Grades: 2 - 4
Pages: 32
Rights: WD

FORMATS

PB: 978-1-77476-900-3
US $5.99
HC: 978-1-77476-899-0
US $24.99
EPUB: 978-1-77476-901-0
US $4.99
PDF: 978-1-77476-902-7
US $4.99
Audio: 978-1-77878-126-1
US $4.99

Chimpanzees

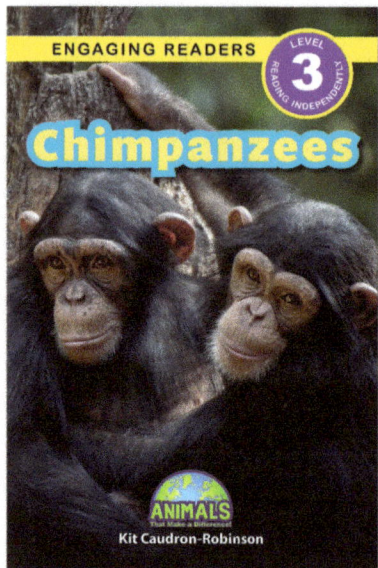

Our closest living relative in the animal kingdom is the chimpanzee. Chimps are intelligent and very social. They like to be with family and friends. Find out how chimps act as jungle gardeners and why chimps are now an endangered species.

DETAILS
Pub Date: August 2023
Size: 6x9 in • 152 x 229 mm
Age: 6 - 9
Grades: 2 - 4
Pages: 32
Rights: WD

FORMATS
PB: 978-1-77476-817-4
US $5.99
HC: 978-1-77476-816-7
US $24.99
EPUB: 978-1-77476-818-1
US $4.99
PDF: 978-1-77476-819-8
US $4.99
Audio: 978-1-77878-133-9
US $4.99

Kit Caudron-Robinson

Cougars

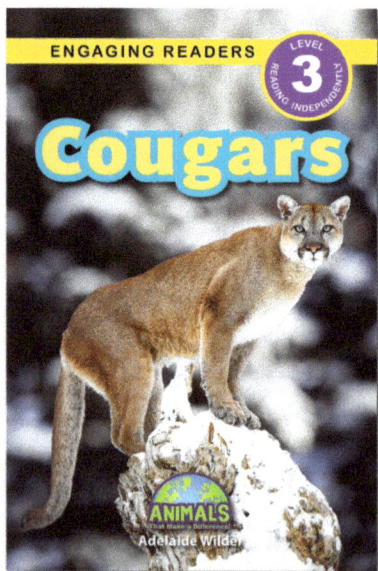

Cougars can be found all across North and South America, but most people have never seen one. Powerful and solitary, cougars prefer to keep away from humans as they hunt and raise their cubs. Find out about the big cat that is known by more names than any other animal!

DETAILS
Pub Date: August 2023
Size: 6x9 in • 152 x 229 mm
Age: 6 - 9
Grades: 2 - 4
Pages: 32
Rights: WD

FORMATS
PB: 978-1-77476-821-1
US $5.99
HC: 978-1-77476-820-4
US $24.99
EPUB: 978-1-77476-822-8
US $4.99
PDF: 978-1-77476-823-5
US $4.99
Audio: 978-1-77878-134-6
US $4.99

Adelaide Wilder

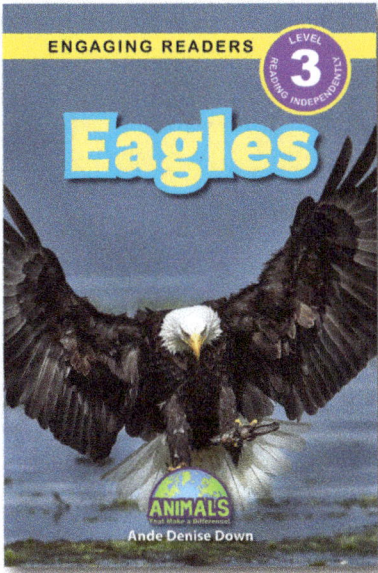

Eagles are powerful birds that can be found all over the world. When they soar in the sky, you can't help but watch. There is so much to learn and love about eagles. Find out what they like to eat, where they have their babies, and how people train them to hunt.

DETAILS
Pub Date: August 2023
Size: 6x9 in • 152 x 229 mm
Age: 6 - 9
Grades: 2 - 4
Pages: 32
Rights: WD

FORMATS
PB: 978-1-77476-837-2
US $5.99
HC: 978-1-77476-836-5
US $24.99
EPUB: 978-1-77476-838-9
US $4.99
PDF: 978-1-77476-839-6
US $4.99
Audio: 978-1-77878-136-0
US $4.99

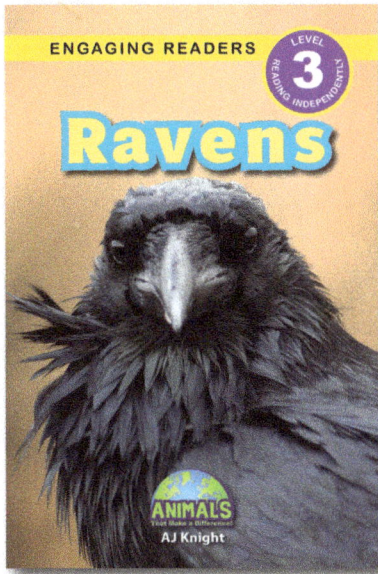

Have you ever seen a bird that looks like a really big crow? It's probably a raven, one of the smartest animals around. Ravens can recognize themselves in a mirror and make over 30 different sounds. Find out why some people call ravens tricksters, how they help their fellow animals, and where you might see one.

DETAILS
Pub Date: August 2023
Size: 6x9 in • 152 x 229 mm
Age: 6 - 9
Grades: 2 - 4
Pages: 32
Rights: WD

FORMATS
PB: 978-1-77476-841-9
US $5.99
HC: 978-1-77476-840-2
US $24.99
EPUB: 978-1-77476-842-6
US $4.99
PDF: 978-1-77476-843-3
US $4.99
Audio: 978-1-77878-137-7
US $4.99

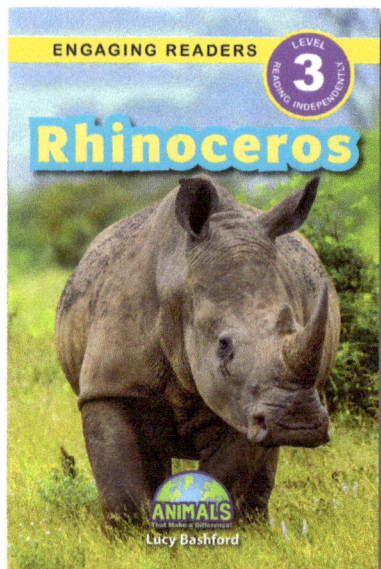

Rhinos look very fierce, but they only eat plants and spend hours grazing, like cows. They even moo when they are happy. There used to be a lot of rhinos in the world, but now they are endangered. Find out why this has happened and what you can do to help save these huge beasts.

DETAILS
Pub Date: August 2023
Size: 6x9 in • 152 x 229 mm
Age: 6 - 9
Grades: 2 - 4
Pages: 32
Rights: WD

FORMATS
PB: 978-1-77476-829-7
US $5.99
HC: 978-1-77476-828-0
US $24.99
EPUB: 978-1-77476-830-3
US $4.99
PDF: 978-1-77476-831-0
US $4.99
Audio: 978-1-77878-138-4
US $4.99

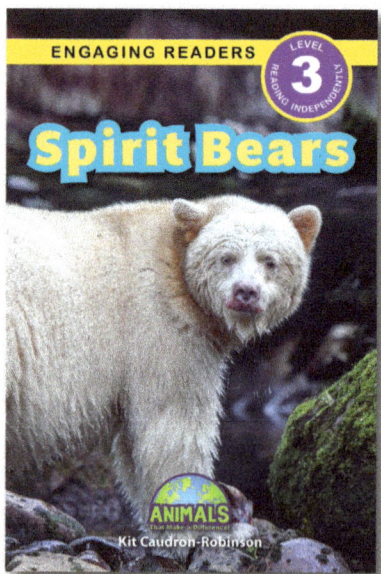

The white spirit bears of the Great Bear Rainforest in British Columbia are very rare. If you are really lucky, you may see them fishing for salmon, climbing a tree, or running through the forest. Spirit bears have inspired people to save the wilderness area the bears live in. Learn how you can be part of protecting this magical bear.

DETAILS
Pub Date: August 2023
Size: 6x9 in • 152 x 229 mm
Age: 6 - 9
Grades: 2 - 4
Pages: 32
Rights: WD

FORMATS
PB: 978-1-77476-825-9
US $5.99
HC: 978-1-77476-824-2
US $24.99
EPUB: 978-1-77476-826-6
US $4.99
PDF: 978-1-77476-827-3
US $4.99
Audio: 978-1-77878-139-1
US $4.99

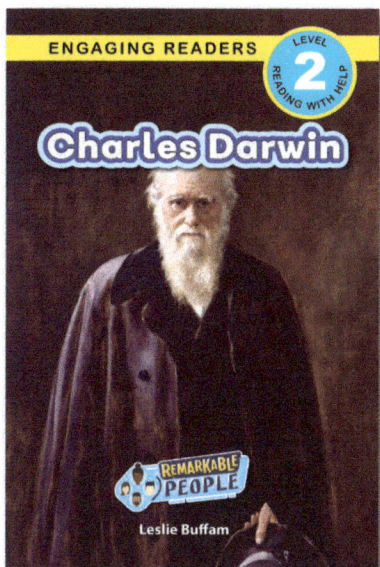

British naturalist Charles Darwin is best known for his Theory of Evolution. His five-year voyage on HMS *Beagle* took him all around the world. Find out how his observations and drawings led him to put forward a theory that shocked and changed the world.

DETAILS
Pub Date: August 2023
Size: 6x9 in • 152 x 229 mm
Age: 5 - 8
Grades: 1 - 3
Pages: 32
Rights: WD

FORMATS
PB: 978-1-77878-309-8
US $5.99
HC: 978-1-77878-308-1
US $24.99
EPUB: 978-1-77878-310-4
US $4.99
PDF: 978-1-77878-311-1
US $4.99
Audio: 978-1-77878-344-9
US $4.99

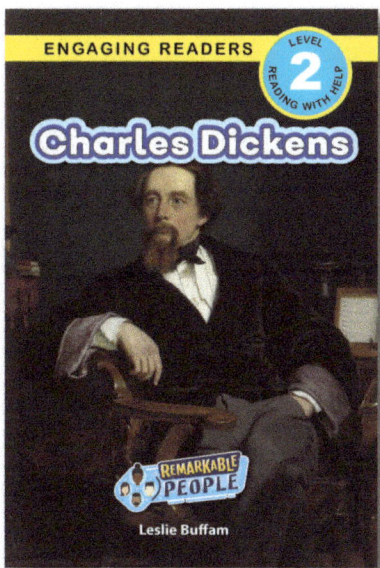

From his humble beginnings to becoming one of the greatest storytellers in history, readers will learn about Charles Dickens' influential novels and his tireless efforts to shed light on social issues. This captivating biography highlights Dickens' vivid characters, such as Scrooge and Oliver Twist, and offers insight into his creative process and enduring legacy.

DETAILS
Pub Date: August 2023
Size: 6x9 in • 152 x 229 mm
Age: 5 - 8
Grades: 1 - 3
Pages: 32
Rights: WD

FORMATS
PB: 978-1-77878-348-7
US $5.99
HC: 978-1-77878-347-0
US $24.99
EPUB: 978-1-77878-349-4
US $4.99
PDF: 978-1-77878-350-0
US $4.99
Audio: 978-1-77878-351-7
US $4.99

ENGAGING READERS
LEVEL 2 READING WITH HELP
Mary Shelley
REMARKABLE PEOPLE
Leslie Buffam

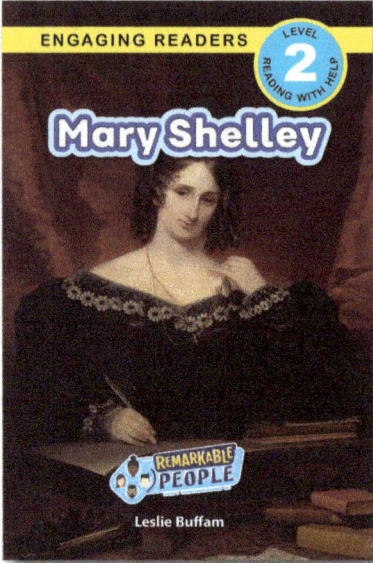

Mary Shelley is a remarkable young woman who penned the iconic novel *Frankenstein*. Readers will discover her upbringing, her creative journey, and the enduring impact of her work. This engaging biography introduces children to the life of a literary trailblazer and inspires them to explore their own imagination and storytelling abilities.

DETAILS
Pub Date: August 2023
Size: 6x9 in • 152 x 229 mm
Age: 5 - 8
Grades: 1 - 3
Pages: 32
Rights: WD

FORMATS
PB: 978-1-77878-322-7
US $5.99
HC: 978-1-77878-321-0
US $24.99
EPUB: 978-1-77878-323-4
US $4.99
PDF: 978-1-77878-324-1
US $4.99
Audio: 978-1-77878-345-6
US $4.99

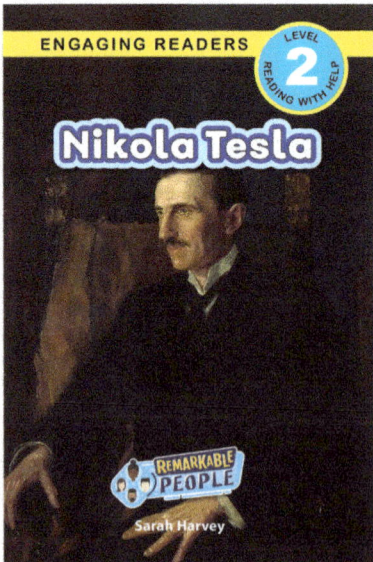

ENGAGING READERS
LEVEL 2 READING WITH HELP
Nikola Tesla
REMARKABLE PEOPLE
Sarah Harvey

Do you watch TV, use a cellphone, or play with remote control toys? If so, then you need to thank Nikola Tesla. His inventions are behind many of the everyday things we take for granted. Find out about his long and interesting life and what he did to become one of the greatest inventors of all time.

DETAILS
Pub Date: August 2023
Size: 6x9 in • 152 x 229 mm
Age: 5 - 8
Grades: 1 - 3
Pages: 32
Rights: WD

FORMATS
PB: 978-1-77476-880-8
US $5.99
HC: 978-1-77476-879-2
US $24.99
EPUB: 978-1-77476-881-5
US $4.99
PDF: 978-1-77476-882-2
US $4.99
Audio: 978-1-77878-346-3
US $4.99

ENGAGING READERS

LEVEL
2
READING WITH HELP

Gratitude

EMOTIONS
and FEELINGS

Karl Jones

Gratitude is a powerful and positive emotion. It can improve your health and help you build better relationships. If you are feeling discouraged, gratitude can lift your spirits. Learn how to recognize the good things in your life and start a practice of being grateful every day.

DETAILS

Pub Date: August 2023
Size: 6x9 in • 152 x 229 mm
Age: 5 - 8
Grades: 1 - 3
Pages: 32
Rights: WD

FORMATS

PB: 978-1-77878-146-9
US $5.99
HC: 978-1-77878-145-2
US $24.99
EPUB: 978-1-77878-147-6
US $4.99
PDF: 978-1-77878-148-3
US $4.99
Audio: 978-1-77878-149-0
US $4.99

ENGAGING READERS

LEVEL
2
READING WITH HELP

Grief

EMOTIONS
and FEELINGS

Sarah Harvey

Grief is a normal and natural response to loss. Each person grieves in their own way. There is no right or wrong way to grieve. There is no timeline or roadmap. Find out about different kinds of grief and how grief can make you feel and act. Learn how to help yourself or someone else through the grieving process.

DETAILS

Pub Date: August 2023
Size: 6x9 in • 152 x 229 mm
Age: 5 - 8
Grades: 1 - 3
Pages: 32
Rights: WD

FORMATS

PB: 978-1-77878-141-4
US $5.99
HC: 978-1-77878-140-7
US $24.99
EPUB: 978-1-77878-142-1
US $4.99
PDF: 978-1-77878-143-8
US $4.99
Audio: 978-1-77878-144-5
US $4.99

LEVEL 2 READING WITH HELP

EMOTIONS and FEELINGS

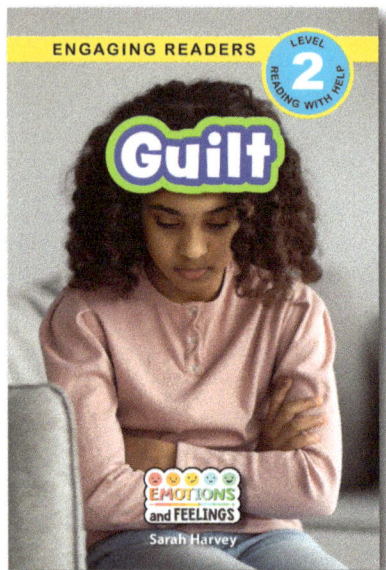

Guilt

ENGAGING READERS · LEVEL 2 READING WITH HELP

EMOTIONS and FEELINGS

Sarah Harvey

When you know you've done or said something wrong, you will probably feel guilty. Guilt can make you feel sad and worried and alone. Learn how guilt can affect your body and brain and get the tools you need to get a grip on guilt.

DETAILS
Pub Date: August 2023
Size: 6x9 in • 152 x 229 mm
Age: 5 - 8
Grades: 1 - 3
Pages: 32
Rights: WD

FORMATS
PB: 978-1-77878-161-2
US $5.99
HC: 978-1-77878-160-5
US $24.99
EPUB: 978-1-77878-162-9
US $4.99
PDF: 978-1-77878-163-6
US $4.99
Audio: 978-1-77878-164-3
US $4.99

Love

ENGAGING READERS · LEVEL 2 READING WITH HELP

EMOTIONS and FEELINGS

Kari Jones

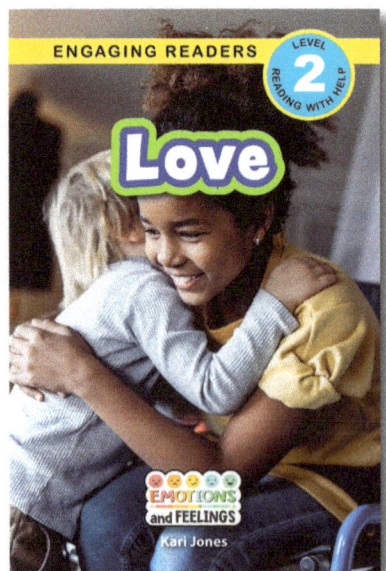

Love is an emotion made up of many other emotions such as joy, surprise, and trust. You can love a person, an animal, or a special place. Find out about all the different kinds of love. Feeling loved and giving love is good for everybody!

DETAILS
Pub Date: August 2023
Size: 6x9 in • 152 x 229 mm
Age: 5 - 8
Grades: 1 - 3
Pages: 32
Rights: WD

FORMATS
PB: 978-1-77878-156-8
US $5.99
HC: 978-1-77878-155-1
US $24.99
EPUB: 978-1-77878-157-5
US $4.99
PDF: 978-1-77878-158-2
US $4.99
Audio: 978-1-77878-159-9
US $4.99

ENGAGING READERS — LEVEL 2 READING WITH HELP

Worry

EMOTIONS and FEELINGS

Kari Jones

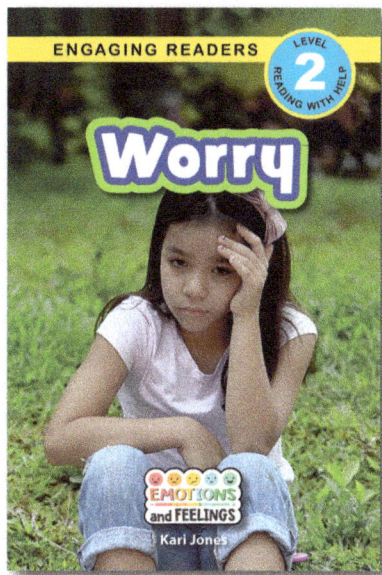

People of all ages worry. Some worry is healthy and some is unhealthy. It can make you feel unhappy and frightened. Sometimes it's very hard to stop worrying. Learn what kinds of things cause worry and how to cope with worry when it happens.

DETAILS
Pub Date: August 2023
Size: 6x9 in • 152 x 229 mm
Age: 5 - 8
Grades: 1 - 3
Pages: 32
Rights: WD

FORMATS
PB: 978-1-77878-151-3
US $5.99
HC: 978-1-77878-150-6
US $24.99
EPUB: 978-1-77878-152-0
US $4.99
PDF: 978-1-77878-153-7
US $4.99
Audio: 978-1-77878-154-4
US $4.99

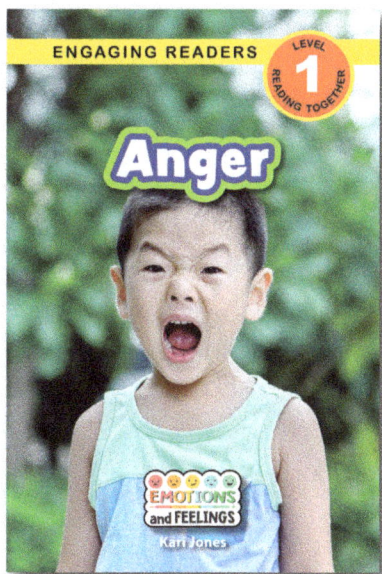

ENGAGING READERS — LEVEL 1 READING TOGETHER

Anger

EMOTIONS and FEELINGS

Kari Jones

Anger is a powerful emotion. Everyone gets angry sometimes. Anger can sometimes be turned into positive action. Find out what you can do to understand anger and deal with it in healthy ways.

DETAILS
Pub Date: August 2023
Size: 6x9 in • 152 x 229 mm
Age: 4 - 7
Grades: K - 2
Pages: 32
Rights: WD

FORMATS
PB: 978-1-77476-797-9
US $5.99
HC: 978-1-77476-796-2
US $24.99
EPUB: 978-1-77476-798-6
US $4.99
PDF: 978-1-77476-799-3
US $4.99
Audio: 978-1-77878-116-2
US $4.99

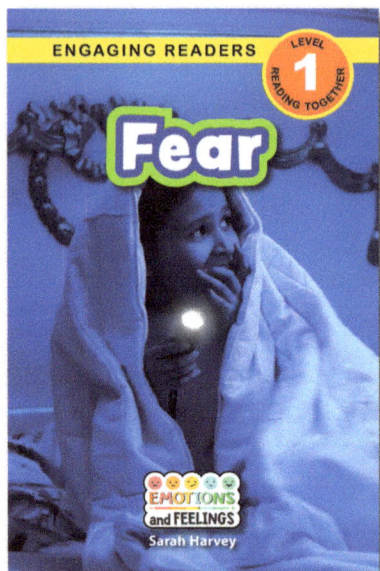

Fear is a strong emotion that is hard to deal with. Very few people like the way fear makes them feel. It helps to understand how fear affects your mind and body. Different people are afraid of different things. Find out what you can do when you or a friend are afraid.

DETAILS	FORMATS
Pub Date: August 2023	**PB:** 978-1-77476-801-3
Size: 6x9 in • 152 x 229 mm	US $5.99
Age: 4 - 7	**HC:** 978-1-77476-800-6
Grades: K - 2	US $24.99
Pages: 32	**EPUB:** 978-1-77476-802-0
Rights: WD	US $4.99
	PDF: 978-1-77476-803-7
	US $4.99
	Audio: 978-1-77878-117-9
	US $4.99

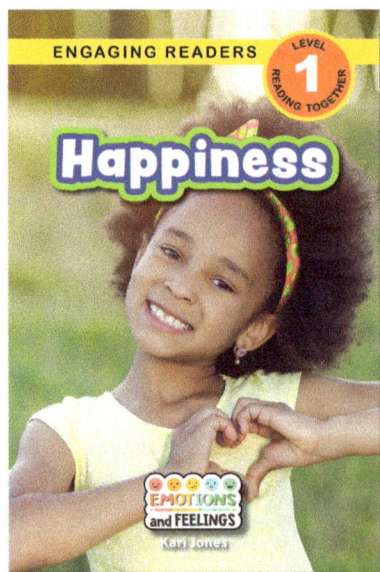

Happiness is an emotion people like to feel. If you know what makes you happy, you can be happy more often. Happiness affects how you think and act, and it can even help change the world one smile at a time.

DETAILS	FORMATS
Pub Date: August 2023	**PB:** 978-1-77476-805-1
Size: 6x9 in • 152 x 229 mm	US $5.99
Age: 4 - 7	**HC:** 978-1-77476-804-4
Grades: K - 2	US $24.99
Pages: 32	**EPUB:** 978-1-77476-806-8
Rights: WD	US $4.99
	PDF: 978-1-77476-807-5
	US $4.99
	Audio: 978-1-77878-118-6
	US $4.99

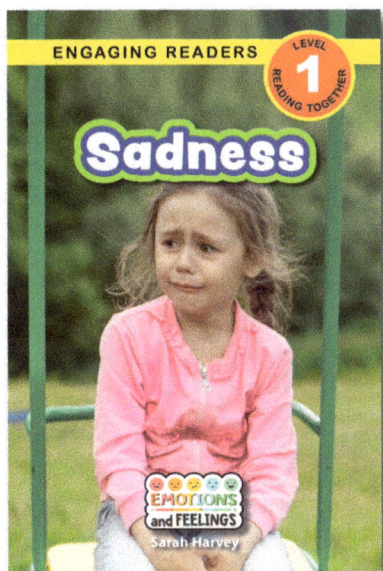

ENGAGING READERS — LEVEL 1 READING TOGETHER

Sadness

EMOTIONS and FEELINGS
Sarah Harvey

Sadness can be hard to deal with. But being sad is a normal part of life. People feel sad about different things. Find out how sadness affects how you think and act and how you can help others who are sad.

DETAILS

Pub Date: August 2023
Size: 6x9 in • 152 x 229 mm
Age: 4 - 7
Grades: K - 2
Pages: 32
Rights: WD

FORMATS

PB: 978-1-77476-809-9
US $5.99
HC: 978-1-77476-808-2
US $24.99
EPUB: 978-1-77476-810-5
US $4.99
PDF: 978-1-77476-811-2
US $4.99
Audio: 978-1-77878-119-3
US $4.99

ENGAGING READERS — LEVEL 1 READING TOGETHER

Surprise

EMOTIONS and FEELINGS
Kari Jones

Surprise is, well, surprising! We often feel surprised but may not know that it is actually an emotion. Some people like to be surprised. Some people hate it! Find out how your mind and body react to surprises and how you might even surprise yourself!

DETAILS

Pub Date: August 2023
Size: 6x9 in • 152 x 229 mm
Age: 4 - 7
Grades: K - 2
Pages: 32
Rights: WD

FORMATS

PB: 978-1-77476-813-6
US $5.99
HC: 978-1-77476-812-9
US $24.99
EPUB: 978-1-77476-814-3
US $4.99
PDF: 978-1-77476-815-0
US $4.99
Audio: 978-1-77878-120-9
US $4.99

Engaging Readers Level Specs

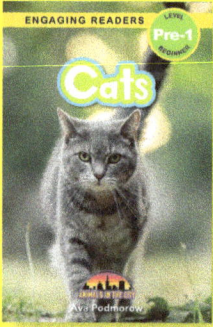

LEVEL Pre-1 — Beginner reader

DETAILS
Size: 6x9 in • 152 x 229 mm
Age: 3 - 6
Grades: P - 1
Pages: 32
Rights: WD

Level Pre-1 readers are aimed at children who are starting to read. Basic language, word repetition, and short, simple sentences help kids read with confidence.

LEVEL 1 — Reading together

DETAILS
Size: 6x9 in • 152 x 229 mm
Age: 4 - 7
Grades: K - 2
Pages: 32
Rights: WD

Level 1 readers are aimed at children who are starting to recognize common words and are capable of sounding out unfamiliar words. Short, simple sentences help guide the reader through new concepts and ideas.

LEVEL 2 — Reading with help

DETAILS
Size: 6x9 in • 152 x 229 mm
Age: 5 - 8
Grades: 1 - 3
Pages: 32
Rights: WD

Level 2 readers are aimed at children who are becoming more confident at reading on their own. Simple sentences and informative captions help readers understand new ideas, while key words increase readers' vocabularies.

LEVEL 3 — Reading independently

DETAILS
Size: 6x9 in • 152 x 229 mm
Age: 6 - 9
Grades: 2 - 4
Pages: 32
Rights: WD

Level 3 readers are aimed at children who are reading by themselves and can grasp new concepts. Key words and captions help readers understand new vocabulary and more challenging sentence structure.

Prices: PB: US $5.99 HC: US $24.99 EPUB: US $4.99 PDF: US $4.99 Audio: US $4.99

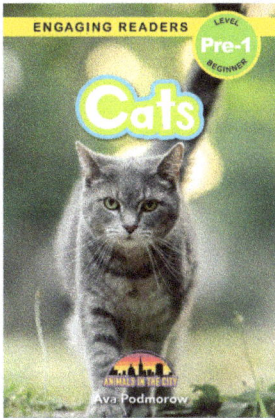

CATS
Pub Date: September 2022
PB: 978-1-77476-757-3
HC: 978-1-77476-756-6
EPUB: 978-1-77476-758-0
PDF: 978-1-77476-759-7

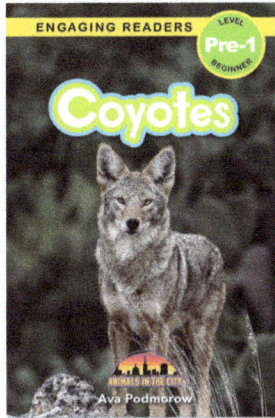

COYOTES
Pub Date: September 2022
PB: 978-1-77476-745-0
HC: 978-1-77476-744-3
EPUB: 978-1-77476-746-7
PDF: 978-1-77476-747-4

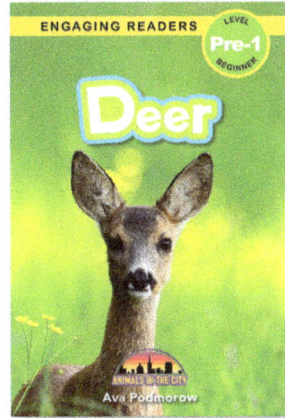

DEER
Pub Date: September 2022
PB: 978-1-77476-741-2
HC: 978-1-77476-740-5
EPUB: 978-1-77476-742-9
PDF: 978-1-77476-743-6

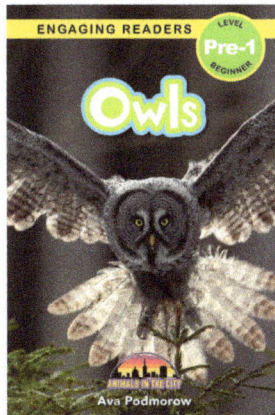

OWLS
Pub Date: September 2022
PB: 978-1-77476-765-8
HC: 978-1-77476-764-1
EPUB: 978-1-77476-766-5
PDF: 978-1-77476-767-2

PIGEONS
Pub Date: September 2022
PB: 978-1-77476-761-0
HC: 978-1-77476-760-3
EPUB: 978-1-77476-762-7
PDF: 978-1-77476-763-4

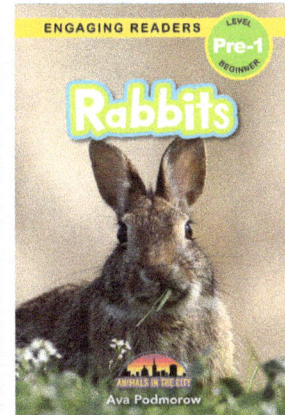

RABBITS
Pub Date: September 2022
PB: 978-1-77476-753-5
HC: 978-1-77476-752-8
EPUB: 978-1-77476-754-2
PDF: 978-1-77476-755-9

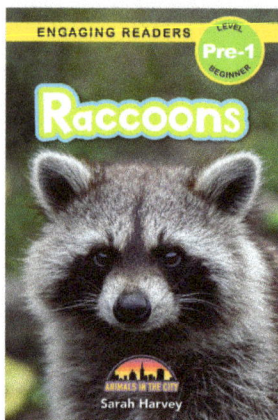

RACCOONS
Pub Date: September 2022
PB: 978-1-77476-737-5
HC: 978-1-77476-736-8
EPUB: 978-1-77476-738-2
PDF: 978-1-77476-739-9

RATS
Pub Date: September 2022
PB: 978-1-77476-769-6
HC: 978-1-77476-768-9
EPUB: 978-1-77476-770-2
PDF: 978-1-77476-771-9

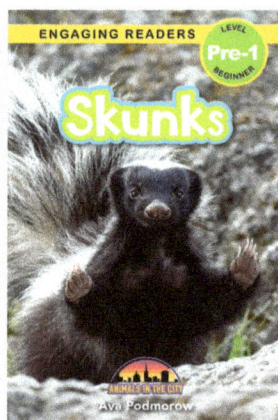

SKUNKS
Pub Date: September 2022
PB: 978-1-77476-749-8
HC: 978-1-77476-748-1
EPUB: 978-1-77476-750-4
PDF: 978-1-77476-751-1

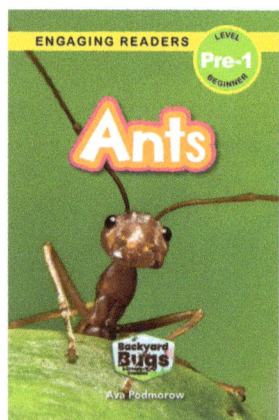

ANTS
Pub Date: September 2022
PB: 978-1-77476-733-7
HC: 978-1-77476-732-0
EPUB: 978-1-77476-734-4
PDF: 978-1-77476-735-1

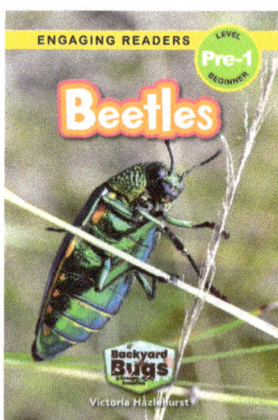

BEETLES
Pub Date: September 2022
PB: 978-1-77476-717-7
HC: 978-1-77476-716-0
EPUB: 978-1-77476-718-4
PDF: 978-1-77476-719-1

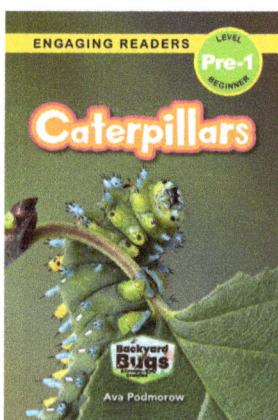

CATERPILLARS
Pub Date: September 2022
PB: 978-1-77476-729-0
HC: 978-1-77476-728-3
EPUB: 978-1-77476-730-6
PDF: 978-1-77476-731-3

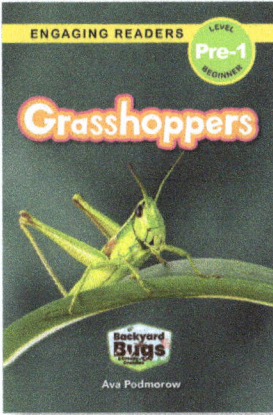

GRASSHOPPERS

Pub Date: September 2022
PB: 978-1-77476-709-2
HC: 978-1-77476-708-5
EPUB: 978-1-77476-710-8
PDF: 978-1-77476-711-5

MOTHS

Pub Date: September 2022
PB: 978-1-77476-713-9
HC: 978-1-77476-712-2
EPUB: 978-1-77476-714-6
PDF: 978-1-77476-715-3

SNAILS

Pub Date: September 2022
PB: 978-1-77476-725-2
HC: 978-1-77476-724-5
EPUB: 978-1-77476-726-9
PDF: 978-1-77476-727-6

SPIDERS

Pub Date: September 2022
PB: 978-1-77476-705-4
HC: 978-1-77476-704-7
EPUB: 978-1-77476-706-1
PDF: 978-1-77476-707-8

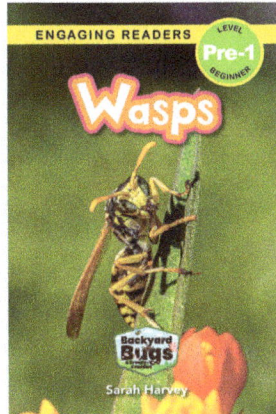

WASPS

Pub Date: September 2022
PB: 978-1-77476-701-6
HC: 978-1-77476-700-9
EPUB: 978-1-77476-702-3
PDF: 978-1-77476-703-0

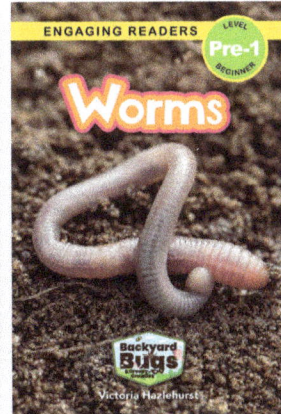

WORMS

Pub Date: September 2022
PB: 978-1-77476-721-4
HC: 978-1-77476-720-7
EPUB: 978-1-77476-722-1
PDF: 978-1-77476-723-8

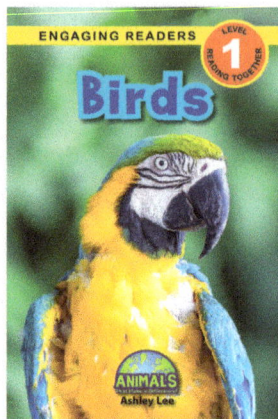

BATS
Pub Date: March 2021
PB: 978-1-77437-673-7
HC: 978-1-77437-672-0
EPUB: 978-1-77437-675-1
PDF: 978-1-77437-674-4
Audio: 978-1-77878-094-3

BEES
Pub Date: March 2021
PB: 978-1-77437-663-8
HC: 978-1-77437-662-1
EPUB: 978-1-77437-665-2
PDF: 978-1-77437-664-5
Audio: 978-1-77878-095-0

BIRDS
Pub Date: March 2021
PB: 978-1-77437-703-1
HC: 978-1-77437-702-4
EPUB: 978-1-77437-705-5
PDF: 978-1-77437-704-8
Audio: 978-1-77878-096-7

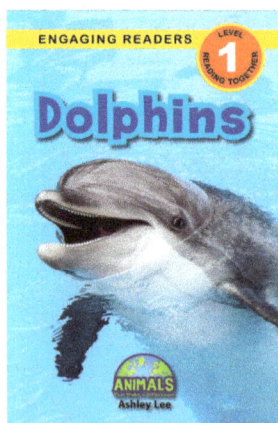

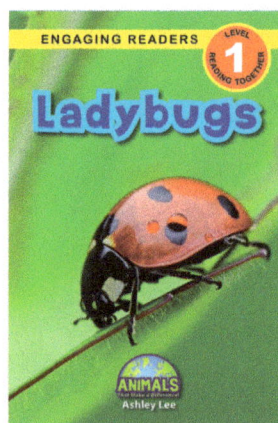

DOLPHINS
Pub Date: March 2021
PB: 978-1-77437-688-1
HC: 978-1-77437-687-4
EPUB: 978-1-77437-690-4
PDF: 978-1-77437-689-8
Audio: 978-1-77878-097-4

HORSES
Pub Date: March 2021
PB: 978-1-77437-698-0
HC: 978-1-77437-697-3
EPUB: 978-1-77437-700-0
PDF: 978-1-77437-699-7
Audio: 978-1-77878-098-1

LADYBUGS
Pub Date: March 2021
PB: 978-1-77437-693-5
HC: 978-1-77437-692-8
EPUB: 978-1-77437-695-9
PDF: 978-1-77437-694-2
Audio: 978-1-77878-099-8

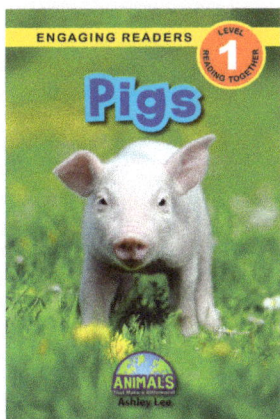

PIGS
Pub Date: March 2021
PB: 978-1-77437-683-6
HC: 978-1-77437-682-9
EPUB: 978-1-77437-685-0
PDF: 978-1-77437-684-3
Audio: 978-1-77878-100-1

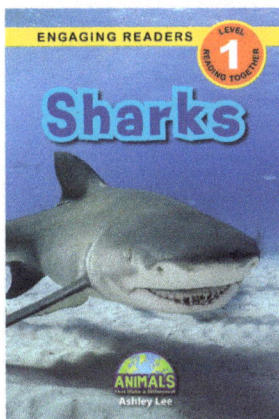

SHARKS
Pub Date: March 2021
PB: 978-1-77437-668-3
HC: 978-1-77437-667-6
EPUB: 978-1-77437-670-6
PDF: 978-1-77437-669-0
Audio: 978-1-77878-101-8

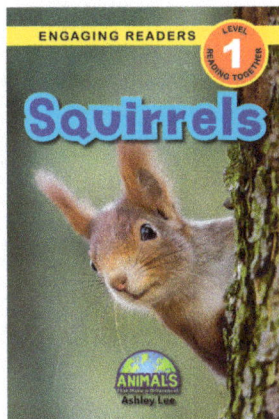

SQUIRRELS
Pub Date: March 2021
PB: 978-1-77437-678-2
HC: 978-1-77437-677-5
EPUB: 978-1-77437-680-5
PDF: 978-1-77437-679-9
Audio: 978-1-77878-102-5

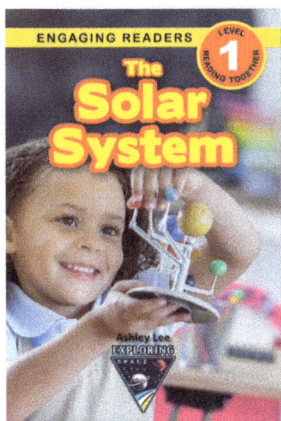

THE SOLAR SYSTEM
Pub Date: October 2020
PB: 978-1-77437-708-6
HC: 978-1-77437-707-9
EPUB: 978-1-77437-710-9
PDF: 978-1-77437-709-3

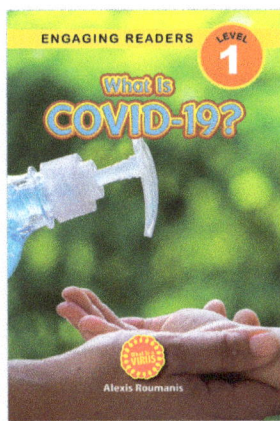

WHAT IS COVID-19?
Pub Date: August 2022
PB: 978-1-77476-665-1
HC: 978-1-77476-664-4
EPUB: 978-1-77476-667-5
PDF: 978-1-77476-666-8
*This book has been edited and approved by the BCCDC.

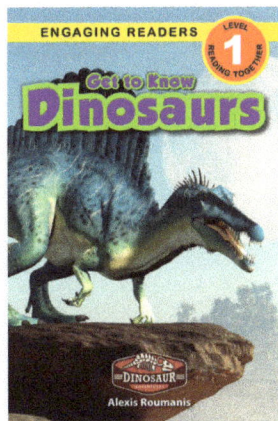

DINOSAURS
Pub Date: July 2021
PB: 978-1-77476-422-0
HC: 978-1-77476-421-3
EPUB: 978-1-77476-424-4
PDF: 978-1-77476-423-7
Audio: 978-1-77878-179-7

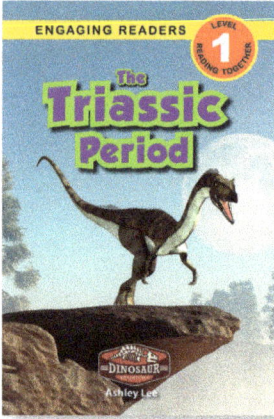

TRIASSIC

Pub Date: November 2021
PB: 978-1-77476-487-9
HC: 978-1-77476-486-2
EPUB: 978-1-77476-488-6
PDF: 978-1-77476-489-3
Audio: 978-1-77878-180-3

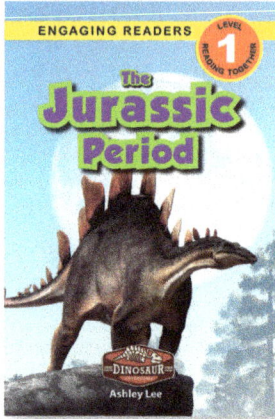

JURASSIC

Pub Date: November 2021
PB: 978-1-77476-491-6
HC: 978-1-77476-490-9
EPUB: 978-1-77476-492-3
PDF: 978-1-77476-493-0
Audio: 978-1-77878-118-6

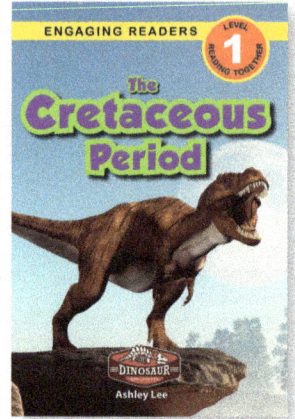

CRETACEOUS

Pub Date: November 2021
PB: 978-1-77476-495-4
HC: 978-1-77476-494-7
EPUB: 978-1-77476-496-1
PDF: 978-1-77476-497-8
Audio: 978-1-77878-182-7

SAMPLE SPREAD

Kinds of Cretaceous Dinosaurs

The teeth of tyrannosaurus rex (*tie-ran-oh-sore-us reks*) were each 8 inches (20 centimeters) long.

Carnotaurus (*kar-noh-tore-us*) is thought to be one of the fastest dinosaurs ever.

The skull of triceratops (*try-serra-tops*) was one third of the size of its body.

Spinosaurus (*spine-oh-sore-us*) is the largest known meat-eating dinosaur at 65 feet (20 meters) long.

Velociraptors (*vel-oss-ee-rap-tores*) were covered in feathers but their arms were too short for flying.

Lambeosaurus (*lam-bee-oh-sore-us*) often lived in groups called herds.

20

21

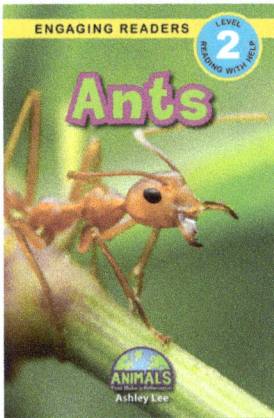

ANTS
Pub Date: September 2020
PB: 978-1-77437-622-5
HC: 978-1-77437-621-8
EPUB: 978-1-77437-624-9
PDF: 978-1-77437-623-2
Audio: 978-1-77878-082-0

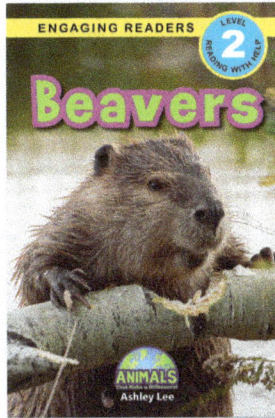

BEAVERS
Pub Date: September 2020
PB: 978-1-77437-637-9
HC: 978-1-77437-636-2
EPUB: 978-1-77437-639-3
PDF: 978-1-77437-638-6
Audio: 978-1-77878-083-7

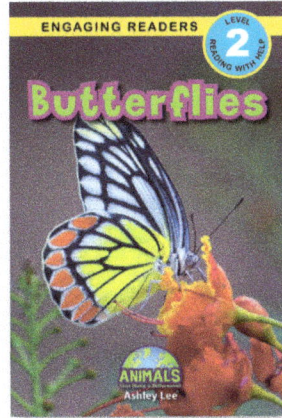

BUTTERFLIES
Pub Date: September 2020
PB: 978-1-77437-627-0
HC: 978-1-77437-626-3
EPUB: 978-1-77437-629-4
PDF: 978-1-77437-628-7
Audio: 978-1-77878-084-4

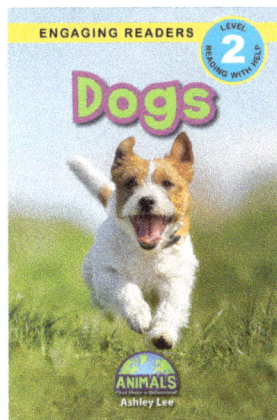

DOGS
Pub Date: September 2020
PB: 978-1-77437-611-9
HC: 978-1-77437-612-6
EPUB: 978-1-77437-614-0
PDF: 978-1-77437-613-3
Audio: 978-1-77878-085-1

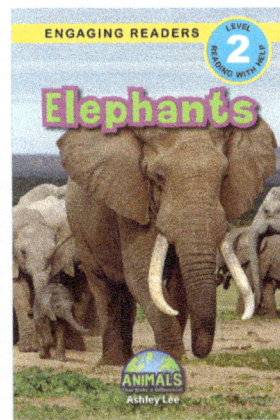

ELEPHANTS
Pub Date: September 2020
PB: 978-1-77437-617-1
HC: 978-1-77437-616-4
EPUB: 978-1-77437-619-5
PDF: 978-1-77437-618-8
Audio: 978-1-77878-086-8

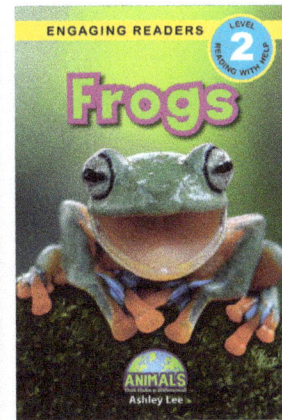

FROGS
Pub Date: September 2020
PB: 978-1-77437-647-8
HC: 978-1-77437-646-1
EPUB: 978-1-77437-649-2
PDF: 978-1-77437-648-5
Audio: 978-1-77878-087-5

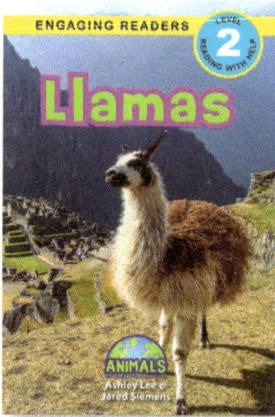

LLAMAS
Pub Date: September 2020
PB: 978-1-77437-652-2
HC: 978-1-77437-651-5
EPUB: 978-1-77437-654-6
PDF: 978-1-77437-653-9
Audio: 978-1-77878-088-2

OCTOPUSES
Pub Date: September 2020
PB: 978-1-77437-632-4
HC: 978-1-77437-631-7
EPUB: 978-1-77437-634-8
PDF: 978-1-77437-633-1
Audio: 978-1-77878-089-9

CATS
Pub Date: September 2020
PB: 978-1-77437-642-3
HC: 978-1-77437-641-6
EPUB: 978-1-77437-644-7
PDF: 978-1-77437-643-0
Audio: 978-1-77878-090-5

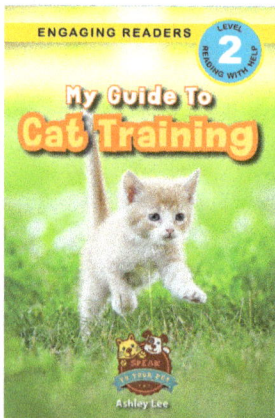

CAT TRAINING
Pub Date: March 2022
PB: 978-1-77476-656-9
HC: 978-1-77476-655-2
EPUB: 978-1-77476-657-6
PDF: 978-1-77476-658-3
Audio: 978-1-77878-184-1

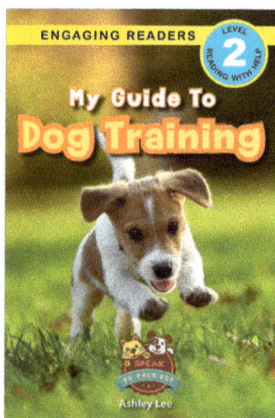

DOG TRAINING
Pub Date: March 2022
PB: 978-1-77476-660-6
HC: 978-1-77476-659-0
EPUB: 978-1-77476-661-3
PDF: 978-1-77476-662-0
Audio: 978-1-77878-185-8

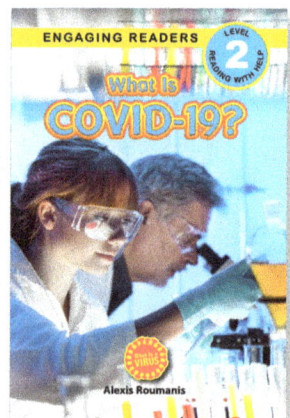

WHAT IS COVID-19?
Pub Date: March 2022
PB: 978-1-77476-669-9
HC: 978-1-77476-668-2
EPUB: 978-1-77476-671-2
PDF: 978-1-77476-670-5
*This book has been edited and approved by the BCCDC.

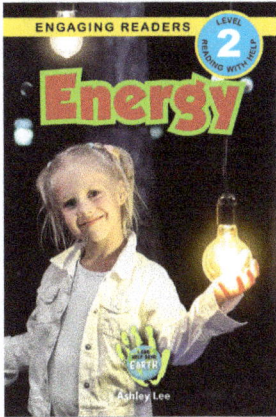

I Can Help Save Earth

ENERGY
Pub Date: March 2021
PB: 978-1-77437-723-9
HC: 978-1-77437-722-2
EPUB: 978-1-77437-725-3
PDF: 978-1-77437-724-6
Audio: 978-1-77878-173-5

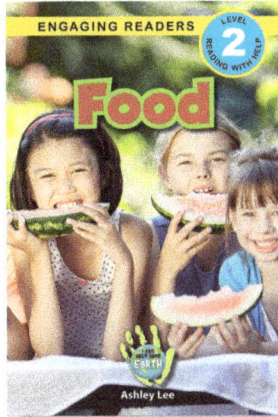

FOOD
Pub Date: March 2021
PB: 978-1-77437-728-4
HC: 978-1-77437-727-7
EPUB: 978-1-77437-730-7
PDF: 978-1-77437-729-1
Audio: 978-1-77878-174-2

GOODS
Pub Date: March 2021
PB: 978-1-77437-733-8
HC: 978-1-77437-732-1
EPUB: 978-1-77437-735-2
PDF: 978-1-77437-734-5
Audio: 978-1-77878-175-9

PLASTICS
Pub Date: March 2021
PB: 978-1-77437-713-0
HC: 978-1-77437-712-3
EPUB: 978-1-77437-715-4
PDF: 978-1-77437-714-7
Audio: 978-1-77878-176-6

WATER
Pub Date: March 2021
PB: 978-1-77437-718-5
HC: 978-1-77437-717-8
EPUB: 978-1-77437-720-8
PDF: 978-1-77437-719-2
Audio: 978-1-77878-177-3

Engage Books Earns Approval from BCCDC

In early 2020, Engage Books created educational books on COVID-19 to help children during the pandemic. We wanted to create accessible resources for parents and educators to help children understand the significant impact that COVID-19 was having on their lives. We are grateful for the help and support of the British Columbia Centre for Disease Control (BCCDC) for helping us ensure the accuracy of our content.

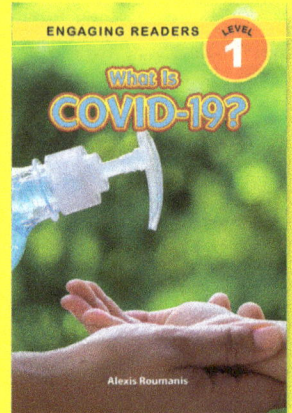

See page 29

During the pandemic, we provided free editions to libraries, the WHO, and various government organizations. In an effort to continue to help children, $5,000 generated from the sale of print editions has been donated to our local elementary school, Tuc-el-Nuit Elementary School. The funds are being used to create an outdoor educational centre for children on the school field. This fits with our mandate of finding creative ways to help teach children about the broader world. We are grateful that our COVID-19 books have helped children understand the pandemic and are pleased that we are able to use revenue generated from these books to continue to help children in a meaningful way.

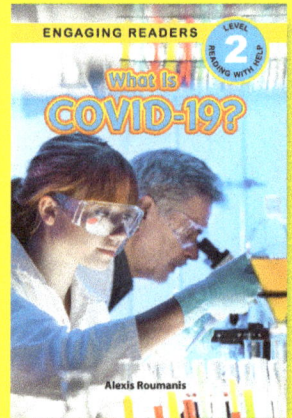

See page 32

Alexis and Dayna Roumanis present Principal Patsy-Anne Takacs with $5,000

THE Toddler's WORKBOOK
LARGE 8.5"X11" SIZE!

LEVEL T AGES 3 - 4

With activities throughout!

ABC 12345678910 Z 123

Alphabet, Numbers, Shapes, Sizes, Patterns, Matching, Activities, and More!

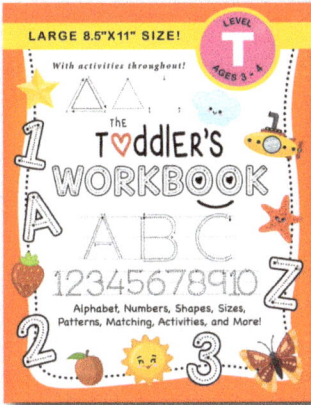

Pub Date: November 2020
Format: Paperback
ISBN: 9781774377710
Price: $9.99
Size: 8.5 in x 11 in
Age: 3 - 4
Pages: 150

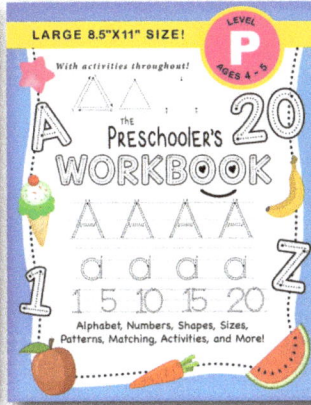

THE Preschooler's WORKBOOK
LARGE 8.5"X11" SIZE!

LEVEL P AGES 4 - 5

With activities throughout!

A 20 a a a a 1 5 10 15 20

Alphabet, Numbers, Shapes, Sizes, Patterns, Matching, Activities, and More!

Pub Date: November 2020
Format: Paperback
ISBN: 9781774377833
Price: $9.99
Size: 8.5 in x 11 in
Age: 4 - 5
Pages: 150

THE Kindergartner's WORKBOOK
LARGE 8.5"X11" SIZE!

LEVEL K AGES 5 - 6

With activities throughout!

Z 20 a a 1 5 10 15 20

Alphabet, Numbers, Shapes, Sizes, Patterns, Matching, Activities, and More!

Pub Date: November 2020
Format: Paperback
ISBN: 9781774377871
Price: $9.99
Size: 8.5 in x 11 in
Age: 5 - 6
Pages: 150

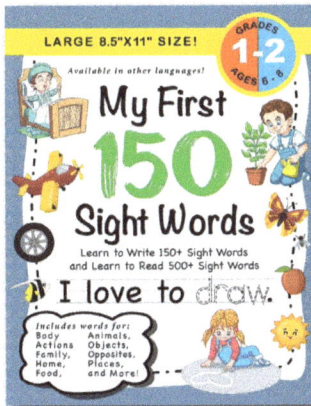

My First 150 Sight Words
LARGE 8.5"X11" SIZE!

GRADES 1-2 AGES 6 - 8

Available in other languages!

Learn to Write 150+ Sight Words and Learn to Read 500+ Sight Words

I love to draw.

Includes words for: Body, Actions, Family, Home, Food, Animals, Objects, Opposites, Places, and More!

Pub Date: November 2020
Format: Paperback
ISBN: 9781774762691
Price: $6.99
Size: 8.5 in x 11 in
Age: 5 - 8
Pages: 70

Table of Contents/목차

TRANSLATIONS

ASL (SIGN)
CREOLE
DUTCH
FILIPINO
GERMAN
ITALIAN
KOREAN
POLISH
PORTUGUESE
SPANISH

Dolphins and Me

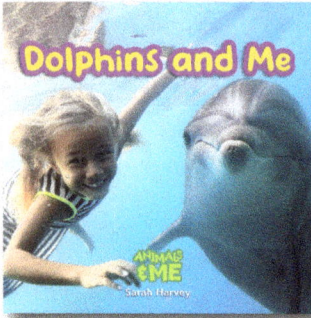

Pub Date: September 2022
PB: 978-1-77476-689-7
US $8.99
HC: 978-1-77476-688-0
US $24.99
Size: 8.5 in x 8.5 in
Age: 2 - 5
Pages: 32
Rights: WD

Elephants and Me

Pub Date: September 2022
PB: 978-1-77476-681-1
US $8.99
HC: 978-1-77476-680-4
US $24.99
Size: 8.5 in x 8.5 in
Age: 2 - 5
Pages: 32
Rights: WD

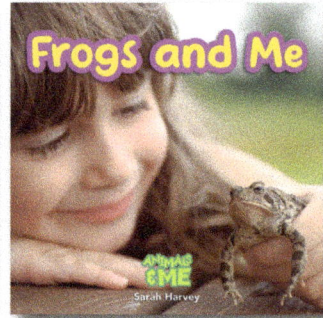

Frogs and Me

Pub Date: September 2022
PB: 978-1-77476-697-2
US $8.99
HC: 978-1-77476-696-5
US $24.99
Size: 8.5 in x 8.5 in
Age: 2 - 5
Pages: 32
Rights: WD

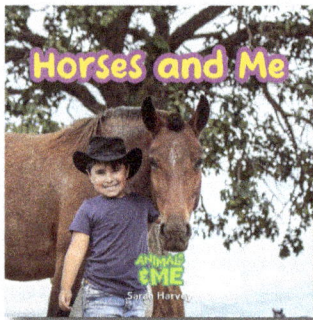

Horses and Me

Pub Date: September 2022
PB: 978-1-77476-693-4
US $8.99
HC: 978-1-77476-692-7
US $24.99
Size: 8.5 in x 8.5 in
Age: 2 - 5
Pages: 32
Rights: WD

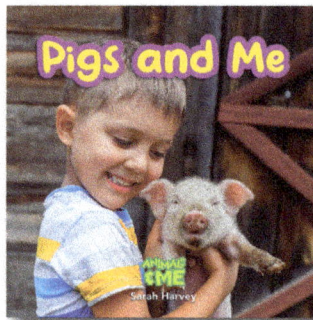

Pigs and Me

Pub Date: September 2022
PB: 978-1-77476-685-9
US $8.99
HC: 978-1-77476-684-2
US $24.99
Size: 8.5 in x 8.5 in
Age: 2 - 5
Pages: 32
Rights: WD

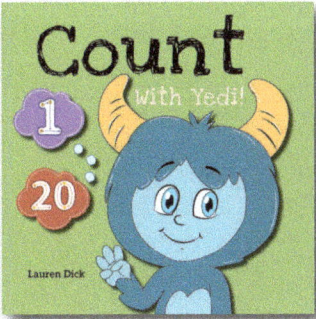

Pub Date: November 2021
PB: 978-1-77476-473-2
US $8.99
HC: 978-1-77476-474-9
US $22.99
Size: 8.5 in x 8.5 in
Age: 3 - 5
Pages: 48
Rights: WD

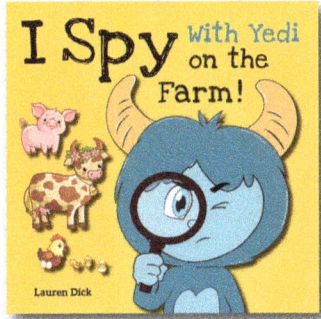

Pub Date: November 2021
PB: 978-1-77476-481-7
US $8.99
HC: 978-177476-482-4
US $22.99
Size: 8.5 in x 8.5 in
Age: 3 - 5
Pages: 48
Rights: WD

Pub Date: November 2021
PB: 978-1-77476-479-4
US $8.99
HC: 978-1-77476-480-0
US $22.99
Size: 8.5 in x 8.5 in
Age: 3 - 5
Pages: 48
Rights: WD

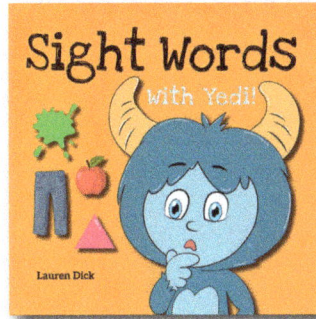

Pub Date: November 2021
PB: 978-1-77476-484-8
US $8.99
HC: 978-1-77476-485-5
US $22.99
Size: 8.5 in x 8.5 in
Age: 3 - 5
Pages: 48
Rights: WD

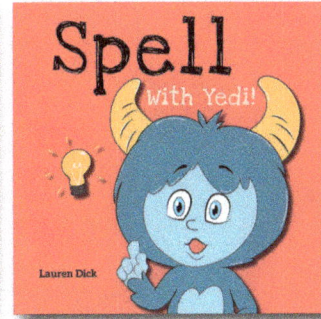

Pub Date: November 2021
PB: 978-1-77476-471-8
US $8.99
HC: 978-1-77476-472-5
US $22.99
Size: 8.5 in x 8.5 in
Age: 3 - 5
Pages: 48
Rights: WD

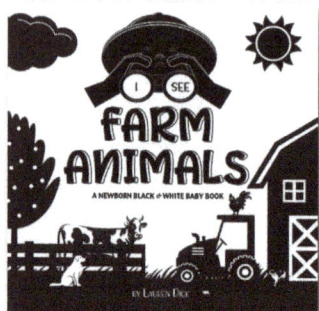

Pub Date: April 2021
PB: 978-1-77476-301-8
US $8.99
HC: 978-1-77476-302-5
US $24.99
Size: 8.5 in x 8.5 in
Age: 0 - 1
Pages: 48
Rights: WD

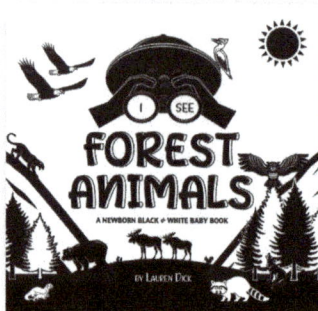

Pub Date: April 2021
PB: 978-1-77476-306-3
US $8.99
HC: 978-1-77476-307-0
US $24.99
Size: 8.5 in x 8.5 in
Age: 0 - 1
Pages: 48
Rights: WD

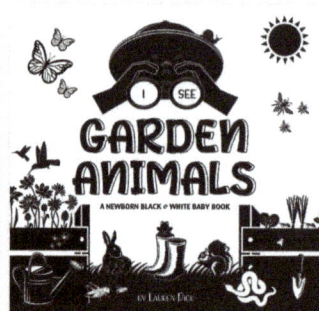

Pub Date: April 2021
PB: 978-1-77476-308-7
US $8.99
HC: 978-1-77476-309-4
US $24.99
Size: 8.5 in x 8.5 in
Age: 0 - 1
Pages: 48
Rights: WD

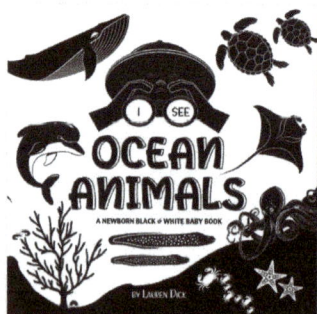

Pub Date: April 2021
PB: 978-1-77476-303-2
US $8.99
HC: 978-1-77476-304-9
US $24.99
Size: 8.5 in x 8.5 in
Age: 0 - 1
Pages: 48
Rights: WD

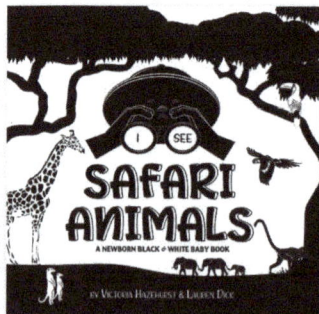

Pub Date: April 2021
PB: 978-1-77476-298-1
US $8.99
HC: 978-1-77476-299-8
US $24.99
Size: 8.5 in x 8.5 in
Age: 0 - 1
Pages: 48
Rights: WD

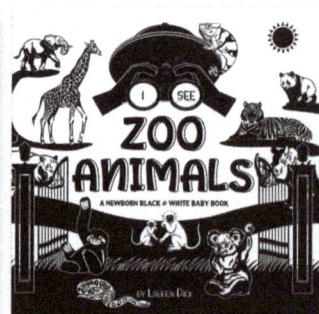

Pub Date: April 2021
PB: 978-1-77476-311-7
US $8.99
HC: 978-1-77476-312-4
US $24.99
Size: 8.5 in x 8.5 in
Age: 0 - 1
Pages: 48
Rights: WD

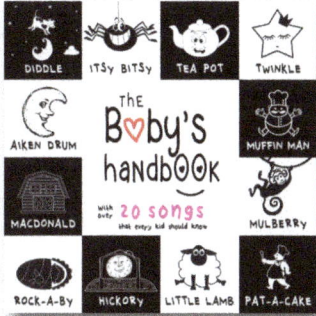

Pub Date: July 2017
PB: 978-1-77226-334-3
US $8.99
HC: 978-1-77226-333-6
US $24.99
Size: 8.5 in x 8.5 in
Age: 0 - 1
Pages: 48

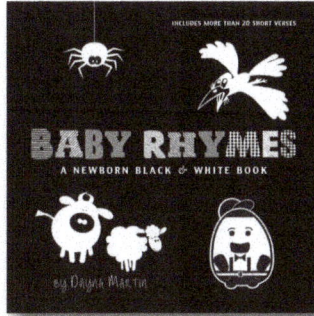

Pub Date: September 2019
PB: 978-1-77226-692-4
US $7.99
HC: 978-1-77226-624-5
US $24.99
Size: 8.5 in x 8.5 in
Age: 0 - 1
Pages: 48

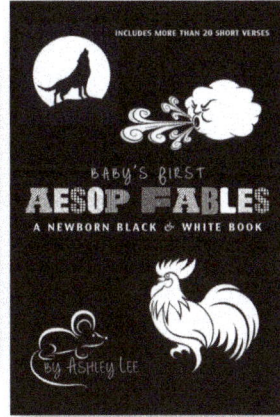

Pub Date: September 2020
PB: 978-1-77437-365-1
US $8.99
Size: 6 in x 9 in
Age: 0 - 1
Pages: 48
Rights: WD

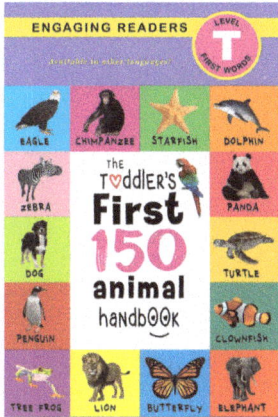

Pub Date: September 2020
PB: 978-1-77437-355-2
US $5.95
Size: 6 in x 9 in
Age: 1 - 4
Pages: 48
Rights: WD

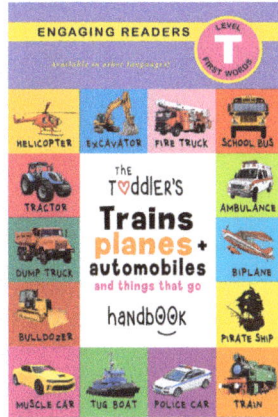

Pub Date: April 2021
PB: 978-1-77437-360-6
US $6.99
Size: 6 in x 9 in
Age: 1 - 4
Pages: 48
Rights: WD

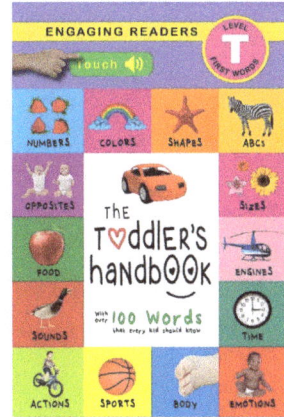

Pub Date: June 2020
eBook: 978-1-77437-350-7
US $14.99
Age: 1 - 4
Pages: 48
Rights: WD

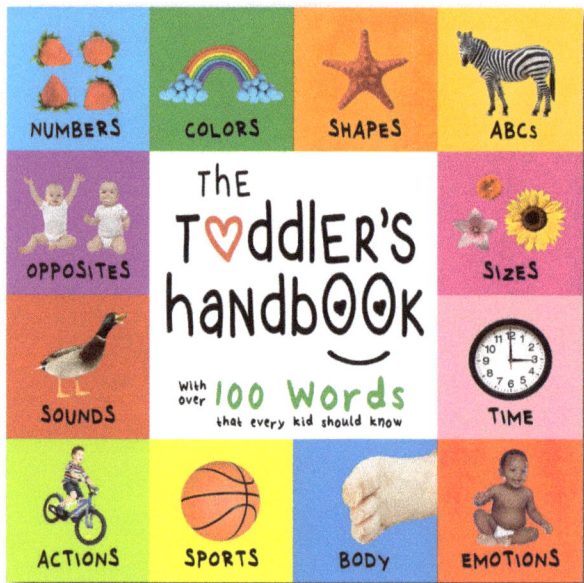

The Toddler's Handbook introduces 17 basic concepts. Included are numbers, colors, shapes, sizes, ABCs, animals, opposites, sounds, actions, sports, food, tableware, clothes, engines, emotions, body, and time. This book develops early language skills using 174 words that every kid should know. Vibrant colors and images are designed to attract the attention of babies and toddlers. This book will help children learn a variety of important concepts before preschool.

DETAILS

Pub Date: August 2015
Size: 8.5x8.5 in • 216x216 mm
Age: 2 - 4
Pages: 48
Rights: WD

FORMATS

PB: 978-1-77226-444-9
US $7.99
HC: 978-1-77226-443-2
US $19.99
EPUB: 978-1-77226-108-0
US $4.99
Advanced EPUB:
978-1-77437-350-7
US $14.99
PDF: 9781772261073
US $4.99

TRANSLATIONS

ASL (SIGN)	ITALIAN
ARABIC	JAPANESE
DUTCH	KOREAN
ENGLISH	MANDARIN
FILIPINO	POLISH
FRENCH	PORTUGUESE
GERMAN	PUNJABI
GREEK	RUSSIAN
HEBREW	SPANISH
HINDI	VIETNAMESE

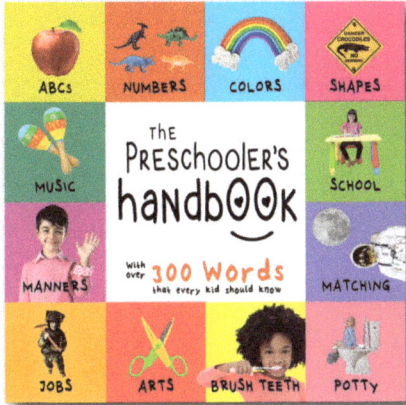

DETAILS
Pub Date: June 2017
Size: 8.5x8.5 in •
216 x 216 mm
Age: 3 - 5
Pages: 48
Rights: WD

FORMATS
PB: 978-1-77226-324-4
US $7.99
HC: 978-1-77226-323-7
US $19.99
EPUB: 978-1-77226-326-8
US $4.99
PDF: 978-1-77226-325-1
US $4.99

The Preschooler's Handbook introduces 18 basic concepts. Included are ABCs, numbers, colors, matching, shapes, school, manners, arts, playground, gardening, biking, car rides, shopping, jobs, potty, and brushing teeth. This book develops early language skills using more than 300 words that every kid should know. Preschooler's will learn to match uppercase letters with their lowercase counterparts, and develop early counting skills. Vibrant colors and images are designed to attract the attention of children. This book will help your child learn a variety of important concepts before kindergarten.

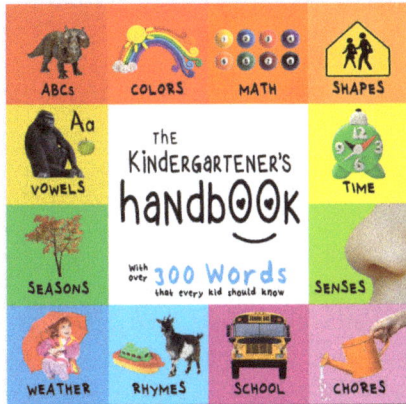

DETAILS
Pub Date: July 2017
Size: 8.5x8.5 in •
216 x 216 mm
Age: 3 - 5
Pages: 48
Rights: WD

FORMATS
PB: 978-1-77226-329-9
US $7.99
HC: 978-1-77226-328-2
US $19.99
EPUB: 978-1-77226-331-2
US $4.99
PDF: 978-1-77226-330-5
US $4.99

The Kindergartener's Handbook introduces 19 basic concepts. Included are ABCs, vowels, numbers, less and more, patterns, shapes, colors, time, seasons, the calendar, senses, rhymes, habitat, weather, chores, and school. This book develops language and reading skills using more than 300 words that every kid should know. Simple words are used to help children read on their own, and more complicated words are presented to help them expand their vocabulary. Vibrant colors and images are designed to keep the attention of children. This book will help your child learn a variety of important concepts before first grade.

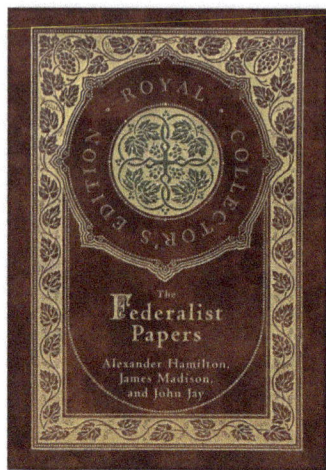

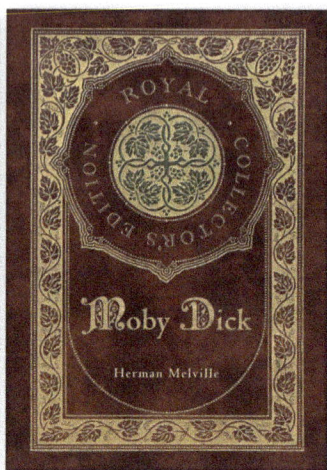

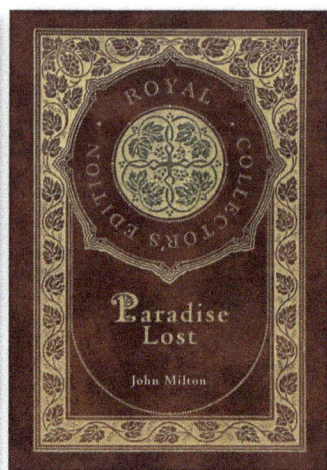

DETAILS

Size: 6x9 in · 152 x 229 mm

Format: Case Laminate Hardcover with Jacket

Text Size: Text is set in 10.7 over 13. A 10.7 point font gives us an average of 66 characters per line of text, which is the optimal number of characters according to Robert Bringhurst's text *The Elements of Typographic Style*. Size 13 leading is used to increase readability between lines of text.

Catalog Numbers: Unique record identifiers on copyright page

Text Design: We avoid widows and orphans. We ensure that there is sufficient white space at the end of paragraphs. This is especially important on text-heavy pages so that the eye can breathe. We set *italic* text throughout our books. All numbers are changed to SMALL CAPS.

20,000 Leagues Under the Sea BY JULES VERNE

A Christmas Carol BY CHARLES DICKENS

A Christmas Carol and Other Christmas Stories BY CHARLES DICKENS

A Connecticut Yankee in King Arthur's Court BY MARK TWAIN

A Doll's House BY HENRIK IBSEN

A Hero of Our Time BY MIKHAIL LERMONTOV

A History of New York BY WASHINGTON IRVING

A Journal of the Plague Year BY DANIEL DEFOE

A Passage to India BY E. M. FORSTER

A Portrait of the Artist as a Young Man BY JAMES JOYCE

A Room with a View BY E. M. FORSTER

A Study in Scarlet BY ARTHUR CONAN DOYLE

A Tale of Two Cities BY CHARLES DICKENS

Aesop's Fables BY AESOP

Against Nature (A Rebours) BY JORIS-KARL HUYSMANS

Agnes Grey BY ANNE BRONTË

Alice in Wonderland BY LEWIS CARROLL

American Indian Stories and Old Indian Legends BY ZITKÁLA-ŠÁ

An American Tragedy BY THEODORE DREISER

Anabasis BY XENOPHON

Anna Karenina BY LEO TOLSTOY

Anne of Avonlea BY LUCY MAUD MONTGOMERY

Anne of Green Gables BY LUCY MAUD MONTGOMERY

Apologia Pro Vita Sua BY JOHN HENRY NEWMAN

Around the World in 80 Days BY JULES VERNE

As a Man Thinketh BY JAMES ALLEN

Au Bonheur des Dames BY ÉMILE ZOLA

Autobiography of a Yogi by Paramahansa Yogananda

Barnaby Rudge by Charles Dickens

Bel Ami by Guy de Maupassant

Ben-Hur by Lew Wallace

Beyond Good and Evil by Friedrich Nietzsche

Billy Budd, Sailor by Herman Melville

Black Beauty by Anna Sewell

Bleak House by Charles Dickens

Candide by Voltaire

Captain Blood by Rafael Sabatini

Catiline's War, and The Jurgurthine War by Sallust

Common Sense by Thomas Paine

Confessions of an English Opium-Eater by Thomas De Quincey

Count Magnus and Other Ghost Stories by M. R. James

Cousin Bette by Honoré de Balzac

Crime and Punishment by Fyodor Dostoevsky

Dark Night of the Soul by St. John of the Cross

David Copperfield by Charles Dickens

Democracy in America by Alexis de Tocqueville

Dialogues Concerning Natural Religion by David Hume

Discourse on Method & Meditations on First Philosophy by René Descartes

Discourse on the Origin of Inequality by Jean-Jacques Rousseau

Doctor Thorne by Anthony Trollope

Dombey and Son by Charles Dickens

Don Quixote by Miguel de Cervantes

Dracula by Bram Stoker

Dubliners by James Joyce

Ecclesiastical History of the English People by Bede

Emily of New Moon by Lucy Maud Montgomery

Emma by Jane Austen

Eugene Onegin by Alexander Pushkin

Evelina by Frances Burney

Far from the Madding Crowd by Thomas Hardy

Fathers and Sons by Ivan Turgenev

Five Dialogues: Euthyphro, Apology, Crito, Meno, Phaedo by Plato

Flatland by Edwin A. Abbott

Frankenstein by Mary Shelley

From the Earth to the Moon by Jules Verne

Gargantua and Pantagruel by Francois Rabelais

Gone with the Wind by Margaret Mitchell

Gorgias by Plato

Grace Abounding to the Chief of Sinners by John Bunyan

Great Expectations by Charles Dickens

Grimm's Fairy Tales by Jakob and Wilhelm Grimm

Gulliver's Travels by Jonathan Swift

Guy Mannering by Sir Walter Scott

Hamlet by William Shakespeare

Hans Christian Andersen's Fairy Tales by Hans Christian Andersen

Hard Times by Charles Dickens

Heart of Darkness by Joseph Conrad

Hellenica by Xenophon

History of the Decline and Fall of the Roman Empire Vol 1&2 by Edward Gibbon

History of the Decline and Fall of the Roman Empire Vol 3&4 by Edward Gibbon

History of the Decline and Fall of the Roman Empire Vol 5&6 by Edward Gibbon

How to Grow Old and a Guide to Friendship by Cicero

Howards End by E. M. Forster

Idylls of the King by Alfred Lord Tennyson

Incidents in the Life of a Slave Girl by Harriet Jacobs

Interior Castle by St. Teresa of Avila

Jane Eyre by Charlotte Brontë

Journey to the Center of the Earth by Jules Verne

Jude the Obscure by Thomas Hardy

Just So Stories by Rudyard Kipling

Kidnapped by Robert Louis Stevenson

Kim by Rudyard Kipling

King Solomon's Mines by H. Rider Haggard

Lady Audley's Secret by Mary Elizabeth Braddon

Leaves of Grass by Walt Whitman

Les Misérables by VICTOR HUGO
Letters from a Stoic by LUCIUS ANNAEUS SENECA
Leviathan by THOMAS HOBBES
Little Dorrit by CHARLES DICKENS
Little Men by LOUISA MAY ALCOTT
Little Women by LOUISA MAY ALCOTT
Looking Backward by EDWARD BELLAMY
Macbeth by WILLIAM SHAKESPEARE
Madame Bovary by GUSTAVE FLAUBERT
Maggie A Girl of the Streets by STEPHEN CRANE
Main Street by SINCLAIR LEWIS
Mansfield Park by JANE AUSTEN
Martin Chuzzlewit by CHARLES DICKENS
Martin Eden by JACK LONDON
Meditations by MARCUS AURELIUS
Memoirs of General W. T. Sherman
    by WILLIAM T. SHERMAN
Memorabilia by XENOPHON
Middlemarch by GEORGE ELIOT
Moby Dick by HERMAN MELVILLE
Moll Flanders by DANIEL DEFOE
Mrs. Dalloway by VIRGINIA WOOLF
My Ántonia by WILLA CATHER
My Bondage and My Freedom
    by FREDERICK DOUGLASS
Nicholas Nickleby by CHARLES DICKENS
Nicomachean Ethics by ARISTOTLE
North and South by ELIZABETH GASKELL
Northanger Abbey by JANE AUSTEN
Notes from the Underground by F. DOSTOYEVSKY
Oliver Twist by CHARLES DICKENS
On Liberty by JOHN STUART MILL
On the Incarnation of the Word by SAINT ATHANASIUS
On War by CARL VON CLAUSEWITZ
Orthodoxy by GILBERT K. CHESTERTON
Our Mutual Friend by CHARLES DICKENS
Paradise Lost by JOHN MILTON
Pensees by BLAISE PASCAL
Persuasion by JANE AUSTEN
Plato: Five Dialogues by PLATO
Plutarch's Lives by PLUTARCH
Poirot Investigates by AGATHA CHRISTIE

Politics by ARISTOTLE
Pollyanna by ELEANOR H. PORTER
Praise of Folly by DESIDERIUS ERASMUS
Pride & Prejudice by JANE AUSTEN
Raggedy Ann Stories by JOHNNY GRUELLE
Robinson Crusoe by DANIEL DEFOE
Second Treatise Of Government by JOHN LOCKE
Self-Reliance, Nature, and Other Essays
    by RALPH WALDO EMERSON
Sense & Sensibility by JANE AUSTEN
Sister Carrie by THEODORE DREISER
Sons and Lovers by D. H. LAWRENCE
Swann's Way, In Search of Lost Time
    by MARCEL PROUST
Tess of the d'Urbervilles by THOMAS HARDY
The Adventures of Huckleberry Finn by MARK TWAIN
The Adventures of Sherlock Holmes
    by ARTHUR CONAN DOYLE
The Adventures of Tom Sawyer by MARK TWAIN
The Age of Innocence by EDITH WHARTON
The Agricola and Germania by TACITUS
The Alexiad by ANNA COMNENA
The Antichrist by FRIEDRICH NIETZSCHE
The Art of War by SUN TZU
The Athenian Constitution by ARISTOTLE
The Autobiography of an Ex-Colored Man
    by JAMES WELDON JOHNSON
The Awakening by KATE CHOPIN
The Beautiful and the Damned by F. SCOTT
    FITZGERALD
The Bhagavad Gita by VYASA
The Blazing World by MARGARET CAVENDISH
The Blue Fairy Book by ANDREW LANG
The Book of Military Strategy by SUN TZU,
    MACHIAVELLI & CLAUSEWITZ
The Book of Mormon by JOSEPH SMITH JR.
The Brontë Sisters Collection by CHARLOTTE,
    EMILY AND ANNE BRONTË
The Brothers Karamazov by FYODOR DOSTOEVSKY
The Call of the Wild by JACK LONDON
The Campaigns of Alexander by ARRIAN
The Castle of Otranto by HORACE WALPOLE

The City of God BY SAINT AUGUSTINE

The Communist Manifesto BY KARL MARX & FRIEDRICH ENGELS

The Complete Essays of Michel de Montaigne BY MICHEL DE MONTAIGNE

The Complete Essays of Plutarch BY PLUTARCH

The Complete Jane Austen Collection: Volume 1 BY JANE AUSTEN

The Complete Jane Austen Collection: Volume 2 BY JANE AUSTEN

The Complete Personal Memoirs of Ulysses S. Grant BY ULYSSES S. GRANT

The Complete Works of H. P. Lovecraft BY H. P. LOVECRAFT

The Complete Works of Horace BY HORACE

The Consolation of Philosophy BY BOETHIUS

The Constitution of the United States of America BY VARIOUS

The Corpus Hermeticum BY HERMES TRISMEGISTUS

The Count of Monte Cristo BY ALEXANDRE DUMAS

The Country of the Pointed Firs BY SARAH ORNE JEWETT

The Decameron BY GIOVANNI BOCCACCIO

The Deerslayer BY JAMES FENIMORE COOPER

The Dhammapada BY BUDDHA

The Discourses BY NICCOLÒ MACHIAVELLI

The Discourses of Epictetus BY EPICTETUS

The Divine Comedy - Inferno, Purgatorio, Paradiso BY DANTE

The Everlasting Man BY GILBERT K. CHESTERTON

The Federalist Papers BY ALEXANDER HAMILTON, JAMES MADISON & JOHN JAY

The First Men in the Moon BY H. G. WELLS

The Genealogy of Morals BY FRIEDRICH NIETZSCHE

The Golden Ass BY APULEIUS

The Golden Bowl BY HENRY JAMES

The Good Soldier BY FORD MADOX FORD

The Great Gatsby BY F. SCOTT FITZGERALD

The Histories BY HERODOTUS

The History of Rome: Books 1-10 BY TITUS LIVY

The History of Rome: Books 21-30 BY TITUS LIVY

The History of Rome: Books 31-45 BY TITUS LIVY

The History of the Church BY EUSEBIUS

The History of the Peloponnesian War BY THUCYDIDES

The Hound of the Baskervilles BY ARTHUR CONAN DOYLE

The House of Mirth BY EDITH WHARTON

The House of the Seven Gables BY NATHANIEL HAWTHORNE

The Hunchback of Notre-Dame BY VICTOR HUGO

The Idiot BY FYODOR DOSTOEVSKY

The Iliad BY HOMER

The Imitation of Christ BY THOMAS À KEMPIS

The Importance of Being Earnest BY OSCAR WILDE

The Innocents Abroad BY MARK TWAIN

The Interesting Narrative of the Life of Olaudah Equiano BY OLAUDAH EQUIANO

The Invisible Man BY H. G. WELLS

The Island of Doctor Moreau BY H. G. WELLS

The Jungle BY UPTON SINCLAIR

The Jungle Book BY RUDYARD KIPLING

The Kama Sutra BY VĀTSYĀYANA

The King James Bible: THE NEW TESTAMENT

The King James Bible: THE OLD TESTAMENT

The Kybalion BY THREE INITIATES

The Lady of the Camellias BY ALEXANDRE DUMAS

The Lais of Marie de France BY MARIE DE FRANCE

The Last of the Mohicans BY JAMES FENIMORE COOPER

The Law and the Lady BY WILKIE COLLINS

The Legend of Sleepy Hollow BY WASHINGTON IRVING

The Letters of Abelard and Heloise BY HÉLOÏSE D'ARGENTEUIL & PETER ABELARD

The Letters of Pliny the Younger BY PLINY THE YOUNGER

The Life and Opinions of Tristram Shandy BY LAURENCE STERNE

The Longest Journey BY E. M. FORSTER

The Lost World BY ARTHUR CONAN DOYLE

The Mabinogion BY ANONYMOUS

The Man in the Iron Mask BY ALEXANDRE DUMAS

The Man Who Was Thursday BY GILBERT K. CHESTERTON

The Mayor of Casterbridge BY THOMAS HARDY

The Memoirs of Sherlock Holmes BY ARTHUR CONAN DOYLE

The Merry Adventures of Robin Hood BY HOWARD PYLE

The Metamorphosis BY FRANZ KAFKA

The Mill on the Floss BY GEORGE ELIOT

The Moonstone BY WILKIE COLLINS

The Murder of Roger Ackroyd BY AGATHA CHRISTIE

The Murder on the Links BY AGATHA CHRISTIE

The Mysterious Affair at Styles BY AGATHA CHRISTIE

The Mystery of Edwin Drood BY CHARLES DICKENS

The Nature of Things BY TITUS LUCRETIUS CARUS

The Odyssey BY HOMER

The Old Curiosity Shop BY CHARLES DICKENS

The Origin of Species BY CHARLES DARWIN

The Pickwick Papers BY CHARLES DICKENS

The Picture of Dorian Gray BY OSCAR WILDE

The Portrait of a Lady BY HENRY JAMES

The Prince BY NICCOLÒ MACHIAVELLI

The Prince and the Pauper BY MARK TWAIN

The Problems of Philosophy BY BERTRAND RUSSELL

The Prophet BY KAHLIL GIBRAN

The Red Badge of Courage BY STEPHEN CRANE

The Republic BY PLATO

The Return of the Native BY THOMAS HARDY

The Scarlet Letter BY NATHANIEL HAWTHORNE

The Science of Getting Rich BY WALLACE D. WATTLES

The Secret Adversary BY AGATHA CHRISTIE

The Secret Garden BY FRANCES HODGSON BURNETT

The Sign of the Four BY ARTHUR CONAN DOYLE

The Social Contract BY JEAN-JACQUES ROUSSEAU

The Sorrows Of Young Werther BY JOHANN WOLFGANG VON GOETHE

The Souls of Black Folk BY W. E. B. DU BOIS

The Strange Case of Dr. Jekyll & Mr. Hyde BY ROBERT LOUIS STEVENSON

The Sun Also Rises BY ERNEST HEMINGWAY

The Swiss Family Robinson BY JOHANN DAVID WY

The Tarzan Collection BY EDGAR RICE BURROUGH

The Tenant of Wildfell Hall BY ANNE BRONTË

The Three Musketeers BY ALEXANDRE DUMAS

The Time Machine BY H. G. WELLS

The Turn of the Screw BY HENRY JAMES

The Twelve Caesars BY SUETONIUS

The Upanishads BY ANONYMOUS

The Valley of Fear BY ARTHUR CONAN DOYLE

The War of the Worlds BY H. G. WELLS

The Wealth of Nations BY ADAM SMITH

The Wind in the Willows BY KENNETH GRAHAME

The Wizard of Oz BY L. FRANK BAUM

The Woman in White BY WILKIE COLLINS

Theogony and Works and Days BY HESIOD

This Side of Paradise BY F. SCOTT FITZGERALD

Through the Looking-Glass BY LEWIS CARROLL

Timaeus and Critias BY PLATO

To the Lighthouse BY VIRGINIA WOOLF

Tom Jones BY HENRY FIELDING

Treasure Island BY ROBERT LOUIS STEVENSON

Twelve Years a Slave BY SOLOMON NORTHUP

Ulysses BY JAMES JOYCE

Uncle Tom's Cabin BY HARRIET BEECHER STOWE

Up From Slavery BY BOOKER T. WASHINGTON

Utilitarianism BY JOHN STUART MILL

Utopia BY SIR THOMAS MORE

Vanity Fair BY WILLIAM MAKEPEACE THACKERAY

Villette BY CHARLOTTE BRONTË

Walden BY HENRY DAVID THOREAU

War and Peace BY LEO TOLSTOY

What's Wrong with the World BY GILBERT K. CHESTERTON

White Fang BY JACK LONDON

Women in Love BY D. H. LAWRENCE

Wuthering Heights BY EMILY BRONTË

ORDERING

Copies can be ordered directly from iPage

About Us

ALEXIS ROUMANIS - PUBLISHER
Alexis Roumanis graduated from Simon Fraser University's (SFU) Master of Publishing program in 2009. Engage Books was founded on his master's thesis, *A Lean Start-Up: Building Engage Books as a Publisher in the 21st Century*. Since then, Alexis has edited hundreds of children's books and written more than 100 educational books. His audience includes children in grades K-12 as well as university students.

DAYNA MARTIN - CONTENT DEVELOPMENT
Dayna Martin is the author of *The Toddler's Handbook* series, which are some of Engage Books' most popular children's books. The ideas in her books were inspired by her search to find better ways to teach her children, and her experiences have inspired her to create resources to help other families. Dayna is passionate about developing new content that will inspire the next generation of young readers.

ASHLEY LEE - EDITOR
Ashley Lee graduated from SFU's Master of Publishing program in 2021. Her master's thesis, *Towards a Better Future: How Engage Books Creates Books That Make a Difference*, explores the underlying philosophy of Engage Books. Ashley is a literary editor and children's book author who has a passion for books that tackle social issues. Ashley lives in Canada, where she enjoys volunteering with children's programs.

MELODY SUN - EXECUTIVE ASSISTANT
Melody Sun graduated from SFU's Master of Publishing program in 2020. Melody's thesis, *Changing Catalogues: Understanding the Influence of the OwnVoices Movement on Canadian Children's Book Publishers*, specifically examines how the OwnVoices trend shaped the current Canadian children's literature. Melody was a bookseller and hopes to make the world a better place by bringing high-quality books to kids.

MANDY CHRISTIANSEN - DESIGNER
Mandy has worked as a graphic designer since 2002. Her career has primarily focused on educational books, branding and marketing materials, as well as video production. Mandy enjoys learning new technologies and techniques to push her further in her graphic design journey. With a passion for book design, she thrives in bringing books to life with visually appealing content for kids.

49

www.ingramcontent.com/pod-product-compliance
Lightning Source LLC
Chambersburg PA
CBHW052034030426
42337CB00027B/5003